Montana
NATIONAL FORESTS

Written by
Gary Ferguson

Research coordinated by
Jane Ferguson

National Forests
— of —
America

ACKNOWLEDGMENTS

A special thanks to Dale Dufour and Beth Horn at the Regional Office of the Forest Service in Missoula, Montana, for helping to keep this project on track from square one. And a sincere note of appreciation to all the men and women of Montana's ten national forests who gave so generously of their time and expertise — who shared with me a spectacular slice of the land that they, and now I, have come to treasure.

ABOUT THE AUTHOR

Gary Ferguson is a freelance writer whose science, travel, and outdoor recreation articles have appeared in more than one hundred national publications, including *Travel-Holiday*, *Outside*, *Field & Stream*, *Sierra*, and *Modern Maturity*. He is the author of nine books, including the acclaimed *"Walks of . . ."* natural history series.

Before freelancing on a full-time basis, Ferguson spent four years as an interpretive naturalist for the Forest Service in Idaho's Sawtooth National Recreation Area.

DEDICATION

To Gilman and Virginia, who helped make Montana home

NATIONAL FORESTS OF AMERICA SERIES

Copyright © 1990 by Falcon Press Publishing Co., Inc., Helena and Billings, Montana

Published in cooperation with the Forest Service, U.S. Department of Agriculture.

All rights reserved, including the right to reproduce this book in any form, except brief quotations for reviews, without the written permission of the publisher.

Design, typesetting and other prepress work by Falcon Press, Helena, Montana. Printed in Korea.

Library of Congress Number 90-080470

ISBN 0-937959-72-3

Front cover photo: Trapper Peak, Bitterroot National Forest. MICHAEL S. SAMPLE

Back cover photos: hiker in the Absaroka Mountains, Gallatin National Forest. GEORGE WUERTHNER; osprey landing on nest, Helena National Forest. ALAN AND SANDY CAREY; wood lily, Lewis and Clark National Forest. MICHAEL S. SAMPLE

Title page photo: Thunder Mountain, Lake Fork of Rock Creek, Custer National Forest. MICHAEL S. SAMPLE

For additional copies of this book, write to Falcon Press, P.O. Box 1718, Helena, MT 59624, or call toll free 1-800-582-BOOK.

FALCON PRESS

Contents

The Bull River forms a lush, timbered valley in the Kootenai National Forest in northwestern Montana. In all, Montana's ten national forests contain more than 16.8 million acres of mountains, streams, forests, and grasslands. MICHAEL S. SAMPLE

Introduction

Nature's sweet symphony

No discussion of Montana's natural wonders would be complete without talking of her national forests. Visitors arriving from the west along virtually any point on the Idaho border will be greeted by a national forest — hushed, wet groves of hemlock on the Kootenai; high, rugged stands of western larch on the Lolo; patchworks of sage and lodgepole on the high, windswept plateaus of the Beaverhead. National forests continue to dominate the landscape eastward across the state, cradling virtually every mountain range, as well as countless icy streams that dance down from the high country to form the great rivers of the northern Rockies.

Not until well past the crest of the Continental Divide, at the threshold of the Great Plains, do the national forests begin to give way to other lands. And even then, across much of southeastern Montana lie scattered island parcels of the Custer National Forest — most of them wrapped in loosely woven blankets of ponderosa pine. In all, more than 16.8 million acres of national forest stretch between the state's western and eastern borders — a tract of land larger than the entire state of West Virginia.

In between the national forests of western Montana and the Custer in the east lie the Flathead, Bitterroot, Lewis and Clark, Helena, Deerlodge, and Gallatin national forests — each with its own natural attractions.

These vast forest lands provide more than a pretty covering for Montana. Here lies timber for homes, grass for hundreds of thousands of cattle, and precious metals ranging from platinum to gold. From a recreational standpoint alone, Montana's ten national forests are a virtual wonderland of opportunity. They contain more than 13,000 miles of hiking trails, nearly 2,000 miles of snowmobile trails, 425 miles of cross-country ski routes, more than 200 miles of Wild and Scenic Rivers, 300 campgrounds and picnic grounds, and 13 downhill ski areas. The number of recreation visitor days per year on all of Montana's national forests is estimated at around 8.8 million, or about 1.2 million more than the number for Yellowstone and Glacier national parks combined.

The national forests found their beginnings in a small but extremely significant amendment quietly tacked on to the General Land Revision Bill of 1891, giving the president the power to withdraw western timberlands from any kind of public use or entry. President Benjamin Harrison seized the opportunity to establish six Forest Reserves totaling three million acres. Today, 156 national forests cover 191 million acres.

Public support for the creation of federal forest holdings originally was stirred by the large-scale harvest of timber in the West during the latter part of the nineteenth century and subsequent lowering of water tables in some areas because rain and snowmelt ran off mountains that had lost their vegetative cover. National forest supporters also hoped a public forests system would slow down the destruction of the forests by wildfire.

Fighting fires often proved to be the most demanding job of all for the first forest rangers, as they struggled to quell blazes in remote areas with only rudimentary equipment. While firefighting technology has advanced over the years, stopping wildfires has remained a challenge. In 1988, Montana suffered its most severe fire season in seventy-eight years. Fires sparked that year spread easily in land left dry by three years of drought. By autumn, more than three thousand fires had burned in the Region One fire protection area that covers the national forests, state, private and other federal lands of Montana and portions of Idaho, North Dakota, South Dakota, Wyoming, and Yellowstone National Park. When the smoke finally cleared, nearly 360,000 acres of Montana national forest land had felt the flames.

Many of Montana's national forests also have felt the effects of the mountain pine beetle, which has destroyed old stands of lodgepole pine in acreages far greater than that damaged in the 1988 fires. On the Kootenai National Forest alone, 800,000 acres of lodgepole are expected to be affected before the infestation runs its course.

But fire, disease, and insects have always been a natural part of any large forest ecosystem and have their own benefits. Fires leave highly enriched soils in their wake, and new grass growth benefits both wildlife and domestic livestock. Standing dead lodgepole killed by the mountain pine beetle provides a highly valued source of logs for Montana's log-home industry.

Forest Service managers do their best to prevent large timber losses to such elements as fire and disease.

Happiness is a young fisherman, a nice cutthroat trout, and a clear mountain stream — in this case, a stream high in the Beartooth Mountains on the Gallatin National Forest in southwestern Montana. Montana's national forests contain the headwaters of many major trout streams, including Rock Creek and the Big Hole River, and major tributaries of the Madison and Yellowstone rivers. TIM EGAN

And the effects of such natural processes pale in comparison with the wonders of Montana's national forests. Visitors here will discover a kind of bold, unbridled magic. It can be found on a thousand trails and mountain tops and along an endless braid of streams and lakes and woods.

"Montana is a symphony," former U.S. Senator Mike Mansfield once proclaimed. If so, then surely nowhere is the music sweeter than in the wide, wonderful reaches of her national forests. ■

A black bear mother coaxes her young cub across a stream in the Beaverhead National Forest in the southwestern corner of Montana. The Beaverhead, like all Montana national forests, supports a rich array of wildlife, from large animals such as bears, elk, and moose to small creatures such as snowshoe hares, red squirrels, and pikas. ALAN AND SANDY CAREY

MANAGING A COMPLEX SYSTEM

Driving north out of Yellowstone National Park into the fabulous high country of the Gallatin National Forest or west from Glacier National Park into the lush green woodlands of the Flathead National Forest, visitors may tend to think few differences exist between national forests and national parks. Both offer numerous recreational opportunities, magnificent scenery, and abundant wildlife.

But differences definitely do exist between these two types of public lands. National parks were set aside to preserve outstanding wild areas in their natural state, and strict protection is their primary emphasis. But national forests were created to improve and protect the resources within their boundaries while allowing for the use of those resources. Unlike parks, national forests permit the harvesting of timber, wildlife, minerals, grass—even such items as mushrooms, berries, and firewood—on a controlled basis.

The Forest Service division of the U.S. Department of Agriculture, with headquarters in Washington, D.C., administers the national forests through nine separate administration zones, or "regions." Montana's national forests fall in the Northern Region (also known as Region One). The regional office is located in Missoula, Montana.

Each national forest has its own supervisor, who generally oversees the management of that forest from forest headquarters. A national forest is then further broken down into ranger districts, each headed by a district ranger.

More than 2,100 people currently work full-time on Montana's national forests. Another 1,700 are employed on a seasonal basis. These people peform extremely diverse tasks, stretching far beyond the management of trees. There are landscape architects, archaeologists, and geologists, as well as both wildlife and fisheries biologists. There are range conservationists, hydrologists, cartographers, and soil scientists, along with smokejumpers, civil engineers, and recreation specialists, just to name a very few. Together they make up an impressive resource management team—one charged with the rather formidable task of holding together the integrity of national forest lands against an ever-rising tide of public demand.

The magnificent western redcedar ranks among the largest trees in America. These giants, which are over 150 feet tall and measure close to eight feet in diameter, are located in the 100-acre Ross Creek Cedar Grove Scenic Area, four miles west of Montana Highway 56. ED COOPER

Kootenai

Rich in resources for all

If there is no poem lovelier than a tree, as the poet Joyce Kilmer once wrote, then the Kootenai National Forest must hold the most beautiful collection of poetry in the state of Montana. Nursed by a modified Pacific maritime climate found in few other places in the state, the lands of the Kootenai explode with trees. Fifteen species of conifers alone can be found here, including ponderosa, lodgepole, and juniper, as well as Douglas-fir, Engelmann spruce, larch, and grand fir. The tenacious whitebark pine clings to the high, rocky folds of the Cabinet Mountains Wilderness, while hushed cathedrals of giant hemlocks and western redcedars rise above the forest floor.

The Kootenai, located in the mountainous terrain of extreme northwestern Montana, holds a variety of landscapes for explorers. The pathways that skirt the magnificent 8,000-foot peaks of the Cabinet Mountains Wilderness, as well as the striking collage of cliffs, spires, and canyons at Bull Lake and Marten Creek, provide impressive views. But first-time visitors to the Kootenai would be remiss if they didn't devote at least some of their time to unhurried ambles through its exquisite forests. For a sampling of stately ponderosa — the pine that John Muir said "gives forth the finest music to the winds" — drive the Tony Peak Road southeast of Libby or along Lower Bristow Creek on the western edge of Lake Koocanusa. Hikers will find stands of alpine larch on Northwest Peak in the

19,000-acre Northwest Peak Scenic Area, while grand old firs line the Fisher Mountain-Tepee Lake Trail. The gnarled whitebark pine greets walkers in the beautiful 15,700-acre Ten Lakes Scenic Area. And finally, for a taste of one of the grandest trees anywhere on the continent, head for the Ross Creek Cedar Grove.

The 100-acre grove is one of the loveliest, most ethereal forests to be found in any of the Rocky Mountain states. Its .9-mile self-guided nature trail winds past giant redcedars up to eight feet in diameter and 175 feet in height and passes a tapestry of other plants common to the Kootenai, including mountain maple, hemlock, grand fir, ferns, violets, wild ginger, showy devil's club, and trillium.

Not surprisingly, the profusion of trees here has long made the Kootenai National Forest a top timber-producing forest. Current cuts on this 1.8 million-acre national forest average upwards of 200 million board feet per year — well above the amount harvested on any other Montana national forest. No other forest in the state has the climate to grow timber at the rate the Kootenai does, and high levels of tree harvesting have changed the dynamics of the national forest in several ways. More than seven thousand miles of roads have been constructed here, a number that grows at a rate of about fifty to seventy-five miles every year. Sixty percent of these roads are open to the public, creating popular road-based recreation such as dispersed camping, wildlife watching, and the use of off-highway vehicles.

Timber-related activity also has affected wildlife. Timber harvests have created open areas for elk and

A logging truck travels to a timber harvest on Kootenai National Forest, above. Weather patterns that more closely resemble regions of the Pacific coast than Montana have allowed logging to become big business on the Kootenai. In a typical year, nearly 175 million board feet of timber will be harvested — enough to build more than twenty thousand homes. DEBI OTTINGER

A self-guided nature trail leads through a magnificent stand of western redcedar at the Ross Creek Cedar Grove Scenic Area, left. Some of these trees are more than five hundred years old. Streamside picnic grounds are located next to the parking area. DONALD M. JONES

The spectacular Yaak River takes its name from an Indian word meaning "arrow," referring to how the Yaak cuts like an arrow across the great bow formed by the Kootenai River. DONALD M. JONES

A HIGH COUNTRY RETREAT

In a state renowned for its beautiful high country, the Cabinet Mountains of the Kootenai National Forest stand in a class by themselves. Caressed by the moisture of a Pacific maritime climate, mosaics of trees and wildflowers flourish here like no other place in Montana—from moss-covered cathedral groves of giant hemlock and western redcedar to delicate smatterings of fairy slipper orchids, from pure stands of alpine larch spreading out from the flanks of high mountain glaciers to mats of dwarf willow, glacier lilies, and mountain heather.

The sedimentary rocks visible today in the Cabinet Mountains are some of the oldest in the West, first laid down over 500 million years ago as clay, carbonate, silt, and sand in a shallow sea. Later, intense heat and pressure transformed these components into limestone, quartzite, and argillite, which were then lifted slowly upward beginning about 60 million years ago.

What gave the Cabinets much of their wild, dramatic profile, however, were the great tongues of glacial ice that pushed southward out of British Columbia thousands of years ago. So large were these glaciers that they completely buried the Purcell Mountains just to the north, leaving them with a softer, more rounded appearance. In the Cabinet Mountains, the glaciers did their sculpting only in the valleys, leaving islands of weathered, craggy peaks floating high above the ice.

Much of the mountain range is now included in a 94,000-acre wilderness area. And the Cabinets provide a myriad of delights for those who walk their paths. Visitors can begin in low, moist valleys filled with towering western redcedar and hemlock, then follow footpaths that rise through Douglas-fir, mountain maple, ash, and lodgepole pine, and finally reach magnificent stands of subalpine fir and Engelmann spruce. Trails in the Cabinet Mountains are plentiful. The paths up Cedar Creek and to Leigh Lake on the east side of the wilderness are particularly beautiful, as are the west-side trails to Wanless Lake and along the East Fork of the Bull River.

Hikers should keep eyes and ears open for the wide variety of bird life here, including blue, ruffed, and spruce grouse, bald and golden eagles, water ouzels, western tanagers, warblers, flickers, and kingfishers, along with an abundance of hummingbirds flitting about the high mountain ridges.

Springtime in the Cabinet Mountains Wilderness means fields of beargrass. Other blooms will continue throughout the summer, following retreating snowbanks far into the high country.
GEORGE WUERTHNER

Lake Koocanusa has become an important fisheries habitat, perhaps most notably for kokanee salmon. Kokanee, which are actually landlocked sockeye salmon, swim up tributary streams in November and December to spawn. The female uses her body to dig a shallow depression in a stretch of sand or gravel, where she then lays her eggs. Both adult males and females die shortly after spawning. The fry will emerge the following spring and make their way back to Lake Koocanusa, where most will live for four years before returning to their birth places to spawn. DONALD M. JONES

deer to browse, thus increasing their populations. Animals such as the wolf and grizzly bear are also found on the Kootenai, in undeveloped, isolated areas such as the Cabinet Mountains Wilderness and Ten Lakes Scenic Area. Managing large timber operations in a manner that protects existing wildlife continues to be one of the greatest challenges for Kootenai National Forest managers.

Mining also has enjoyed a long partnership with the Kootenai. In the 1860s and 1870s, thousands of miners poured through the Cabinet Mountains, looking for the elusive glint of gold. Although no big bonanzas were discovered, the Snowshoe Mine south of U.S. Highway 2 in the Cabinet Mountains paid off rather handsomely around the turn of the century, producing well over $1 million in gold, silver, and lead.

With rising metal prices and new technologies that allow extraction of more precious metals from a given ton of rock, the Kootenai is seeing a surge in mining activity. The number of patented and unpatented claims filed on the national forest exceeds ten thousand. In 1988 alone, the national forest approved sixty small-scale prospecting, exploration, and extraction operations. Estimates place the total worth of the Kootenai's known mineral reserves at a staggering $5 billion.

Two silver and copper mines have been proposed on either side of the Cabinet Mountains, with one mine expected to produce ten thousand tons of ore a day for roughly thirty years. Both operations call for construction of underground tunnels up to nine thousand feet in length beneath the Cabinet Mountains

Wilderness to reach silver- and copper-bearing ores. One of the mines would be located under lands that lie within the boundaries of the wilderness itself.

A natural-resource harvest of an edible variety also occurs in the Kootenai. Thousands of people come each summer to fish at Lake Koocanusa, a ninety-mile reservoir that stretches from sixteen miles north of Libby far into the wilds of British Columbia. (The word Koocanusa, incidentally, is a shorthand combination of the words "Kootenai," "Canada," and "USA.") Nearly all of the U.S. portion of Lake Koocanusa lies in the luxurious cloak of the Kootenai National Forest, the east side liberally sprinkled with campgrounds, boat launching ramps, and picnic areas. Kokanee salmon have become so abundant here that in the late 1980s, daily catch limits were raised from twenty per day to forty for a short period. Many a fisherman sets up temporary housekeeping at the Tobacco Plains or Rexford Bench campgrounds, catches the limit of kokanee, and then cans them on the spot, thus assuring a supply of these delectable fish all winter long.

The national forest also offers bountiful crops of mushrooms and berries. Mushrooms can be found near many of the forest's campgrounds and open, grassy areas. Morels, a variety of mushroom relished by even the most discriminating gourmet, often can be located each spring on old burn areas of the Kootenai. An especially large and delicious hybrid morel will be found growing in healthy numbers beneath stands of ponderosa pine and Douglas-fir.

For dessert, there's the Kootenai berry crop — a juicy, mouth-watering explosion of raspberries,

GARY BRETTNACHER

AL BRATKOVICH

Vigorous fire suppression efforts over the past fifty years have reduced the quantity of both browse and grasses that animals such as bighorn sheep, left, need to survive. Forest Service wildlife biologists use controlled burning, right, as one method to restore this important food source.

A black bear, above, fattens up for a long winter. Common residents of Kootenai National Forest, black bears have a diverse diet, feeding on everything from berries and bulbs to roots, insects, and carrion. Bears do not actually hibernate, but enter a deep sleep from which they will awaken many times during the cold months.
DENVER A. BRYAN

A swinging bridge across the scenic Kootenai River, left, takes visitors to views of Kootenai Falls, west of Libby off U.S. Highway 2.
DONALD M. JONES

EPIDEMIC STRIKES THE LODGEPOLE

In many places along the roads of the Kootenai National Forest, visitors can look up and see rusty brown patches of dead lodgepole pine. Most of these trees were killed by the mountain pine beetle —an insect whose population periodically rises to epidemic proportions in the Rocky Mountains and then tapers off for years.

Healthy lodgepole and ponderosa pines can usually repel pine beetles simply by exuding pitch, but trees weakened by drought, disease, or age are vulnerable to attack. Most of the lodgepole on the Kootenai National Forest began life after the severe fire season of 1910 and are becoming susceptible to invasion by mountain pine beetles. In the late summer, these beetles lay eggs between the inner wood and the bark of the trees. The eggs soon hatch into larvae, which feed on the trees throughout the winter months. The following summer they emerge as flying adults, ready to attack other stands nearby. However, the majority of the damage to the trees actually comes from a fungus the beetles carry on their bodies. This fungus, which appears as a dull blue stain spread across the wood, damages the cells that help transport nutrients. Death is relatively quick. A tree attacked by the mountain pine beetle and infected with the fungus this year will be dead by next summer.

National forest officials estimate the mountain pine beetle has killed 500,000 acres of trees on the Kootenai. Before the infestation cycle is complete—probably sometime in the early 1990s— another 300,000 acres of trees are expected to die. That amounts to more than twice the acreage burned on all Montana national forests during the severe fire season of 1988. Other Rocky Mountain forests have had some success limiting their pine beetle infestations through chemical repellents or by cutting "safe zones" around affected timber. But the Kootenai epidemic has proven too extreme for such measures. Instead, previously attacked and high-risk stands of lodgepole are simply logged— currently at the rate of about 100 million to 120 million board feet every year.

The beautiful, but ultimately deadly, signs of the mountain pine beetle appear on a lodgepole pine. These grooves, known as "egg galleries," are caused by female beetles boring underneath the bark of the tree. KRISTI DUBOIS

currants, thimbleberries, serviceberries, holly grapes, huckleberries, and strawberries. Huckleberries can be especially profuse here. During a good year, pickers can head out to an old burn or clearcut and gather to their heart's content. Experienced pickers will easily fill a gallon bucket in less than an hour. Huckleberries growing in the lower elevations of the Cabinet Mountains are usually ready for eating in late July and August, and those in higher areas — such as the tributaries of the beautiful Yaak and Upper Vermillion rivers — can be harvested several weeks later. The berries are still available until late September in the higher reaches of the Ten Lakes Scenic Area.

The Kootenai also offers visitors more than 1,300 miles of trails. Ambitious hikers can tackle the 23-mile Skyline Mountain Trail, which runs from near Libby to the lovely Yaak River Valley, or the 22-mile Trout Creek Loop Trail, which courses through the lush flanks of the Purcell Mountains. Visitors to the west side of Lake Koocanusa should take in the short, cool stroll to Little North Fork Falls — a handicapped-accessible walk just west of Forest Road 228.

Collecting mushrooms, like this tasty morel above, is a favorite activity of spring visitors to the Kootenai National Forest. Recently burned areas provide one of the best places to locate morels, because moist mineral soils and ash create ideal growing conditions. STEVE WIRT

Since becoming part of the National Wilderness Preservation system in 1964, the rugged Cabinet Mountains Wilderness has become a favorite with hikers and backpackers, left. The hiking season tends to be short, however, as snowstorms can hit as late as June or as early as September. MICHAEL S. SAMPLE

The Kootenai has been, and will continue to be, Montana's premier timber-producing forest. Yet scattered among the logging areas are a hundred wild nooks and crannies that beckon the angler, hunter, hiker, canoeist, berry picker, skier, and snowmobiler.

It's in these lush protected areas that visitors can gain a real sense of what Longfellow meant when he wrote of the forest primeval — that kind of secret, hushed place, where "the murmuring pines and the hemlocks, stand like Druids of old." ■

An osprey guards its recent catch, a spawning kokanee salmon from Lake Koocanusa in the Kootenai National Forest. Vast numbers of kokanee provide an important food source for many animals, including eagles, bears, and weasels. Even people — in the form of eager fishermen — delight in the salmon's rich taste. M. WICKES

KOOTENAI
NATIONAL FOREST DIRECTORY

POINTS OF INTEREST

LAKE KOOCANUSA is a 90-mile reservoir formed by Libby Dam, seventeen miles northeast of Libby.

ROSS CREEK CEDAR GROVE SCENIC AREA contains giant redcedars and an easily traveled interpretive trail. The 100-acre grove is located off Montana Highway 56, southwest of Libby.

NORTHWEST PEAK SCENIC AREA in the northwest corner of the Kootenai can be reached by forest roads off of U.S. Highway 2 and Montana Highway 508. The Northwest Peak Trail offers views into the West Fork of the Yaak River drainage.

TEN LAKES SCENIC AREA contains glacier-scoured highlands sheltering a fine collection of alpine lakes. Located in the northeastern corner of the forest along the Canadian border.

KOOTENAI FALLS is a scenic attraction on the Kootenai River adjacent to U.S. Highway 2, between Libby and Troy. The river drops ninety feet in less than a mile here.

NOXON AND CABINET GORGE RESERVOIRS lie only a few miles apart, along Montana Highway 200 in the scenic Clark Fork River Valley. Good bass fishing in the Noxon Reservoir and edible crayfish in the Cabinet Gorge Reservoir.

WILDERNESS AREAS

CABINET MOUNTAINS 94,272 acres of rugged lands, with hemlock and western redcedar stands in valley bottoms and alpine plant communities at the higher elevations.

RECREATIONAL OPPORTUNITIES

HIKING AND RIDING 1,410 miles of trails, including five National Recreation Trails. Excellent opportunities for dayhiking and two-day trips. The remote Selkirk Mountains can be reached by a handful of trails in the 19,100-acre Northwest Peaks Scenic Area.

CAMPING Thirty-five campgrounds, most open from late April or early May through September. Dispersed camping allowed on much of the forest.

RECREATIONAL CABINS Five fire lookouts and one lookout/cabin available for rent. For more information, contact the Forest Supervisor's office.

SCENIC DRIVES Montana Highway 56, which runs along the west side of the Cabinet Mountains Wilderness, presents beautiful vistas of the Cabinet Mountains and Scotchman's Peak as it winds the entire length of the Bull River. Scenic views along the Yaak River can be seen from Montana Highway 508 and Forest Development Highway 92.

KAYAKING AND CANOEING Both kayaking and canoeing are popular on the Kootenai River below Libby Dam. The Yaak River can be floated from Upper Ford to Whitetail Creek and the Fisher River from U.S. Highway 2 to the Wolf Creek junction. All rivers are best run from late spring through early summer.

HUNTING Moose, elk, deer, mountain goat, bighorn sheep, and black bear.

FISHING Renowned kokanee salmon fishing on Lake Koocanusa. Many low-elevation lakes contain rainbow, cutthroat, brook, and lake trout, as well as largemouth bass, northern pike, and yellow perch. Most high country streams and lakes have trout populations.

ALPINE SKIING Turner Mountain Ski Area (one T-bar), located twenty-two miles north of Libby.

CROSS-COUNTRY SKIING Good opportunities on roads and trails throughout the forest.

SNOWMOBILING Good opportunities in various areas of the forest. More than thirty miles of marked trails in the Purcell Mountains north of Libby and several routes near Troy.

OFF-ROAD VEHICLES A popular trail bike area is Sheldon Flats, located 1.5 miles north of Libby on Forest Road 68. Off-highway vehicle spots along Lake Koocanusa. Mountain biking allowed on more than 2,500 miles of closed roads throughout the Kootenai and along portions of "Old Highway 2," six miles west of Libby off the current U.S. Highway 2.

ADMINISTRATIVE OFFICES

FOREST HEADQUARTERS 506 U.S. Highway 2 West, Libby, MT 59923 (406) 293-6211

LIBBY RANGER DISTRICT 1263 Highway 37, Libby, MT 59923 (406) 293-7741

FISHER RIVER RANGER DISTRICT 12557 Highway 37, Libby, MT 59874 (406) 293-7773

REXFORD RANGER DISTRICT P.O. Box 666, Eureka, MT 59917 (406) 296-2536

FORTINE RANGER DISTRICT P.O. Box 116, Fortine, MT 59918 (406) 882-4451

THREE RIVERS RANGER DISTRICT 1437 North Highway 2, Troy, MT 59935 (406) 295-4693

CABINET RANGER DISTRICT HCR 2 Box 210, Trout Creek, MT 59874 (406) 847-2462

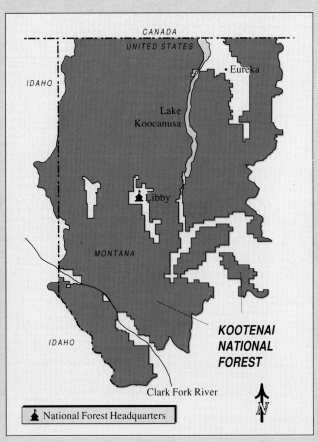

The deep canyons of the Swan Range, on the Flathead National Forest, were formed partly by the grinding action of glacial ice during the Pleistocene era. LARRY MAYER

Flathead

N A T I O N A L F O R E S T

A natural playground

Try to conjure up a picture of the most exquisite Rocky Mountain high country imaginable — great, unbroken reaches of alpine meadows, towering peaks, rivers, sparkling lakes, and wildlife of every kind. Any such daydream likely would fall short of the beauty of northwest Montana's Flathead National Forest. Encircled by other national forests and protected lands, the Flathead is the true heart of the northern Rocky Mountain wild lands. Forty-seven percent of the Flathead's 2.3 million acres is congressionally designated wilderness — a source of unlimited inspiration to humans and a snug, wild harbor for wolves, peregrine falcons, bald eagles, and grizzly bears. Grizzlies, in fact, occupy fully eighty-seven percent of Flathead National Forest lands.

Bird watchers will be especially delighted with the Flathead, where more than two hundred species have been recorded. Wetlands, ponds, and lakes are scattered throughout the forest, providing refuge to such waterfowl as merganser, blue-winged teal, great blue heron, mallard, goldeneye, and horned grebe. Other birds frequently spotted include the ruby-crowned kinglet, pine siskin, bald eagle, yellow-bellied sapsucker, and dark-eyed junco.

The diversity of life on the Flathead is as striking as the sheer immensity of the region. Precipitation on this national forest ranges from twenty inches to sixty inches annually. The moisture creates widely varying zones of plant life, from lush groves of cedars cloaked in moss to lone whitebark pines clinging to the tops of windswept mountain ridges. Likewise, the landforms themselves vary greatly — from the magnificent 74,000-acre Mission Mountains Wilderness with its craggy reaches of bare rock to the thick green pockets of maple, willow, and birch that lie scattered across the northern edge of the Bob Marshall Wilderness.

The Flathead and adjacent undeveloped lands, including Glacier and Waterton national parks, create a recreational wonderland nearly ten thousand square miles in size, or roughly equivalent to the size of Vermont.

Fortunately, getting into this country is relatively easy. Nearly 2,100 miles of foot and horse trails cross the Flathead National Forest, almost equaling all of the forest's primary roads put together. Some fantastic long trips can be made here, such as the seventy- to one hundred-mile loops branching out from beautiful Holland Lake, just east of Montana Highway 83.

Sunset falls on the rugged metamorphic rocks of the Mission Mountains Wilderness. Portions of this wilderness were once frequented by Flathead and Pend Oreille Indians, who came here to hunt, fish, and collect wild plants. Today, about forty-five miles of Forest Service trails wind through the Mission Mountains. DALE J. DUFOUR

One of Montana's rarest animals, the gray wolf, above, may be found in the wildest reaches of Flathead National Forest. This national forest currently provides habitat for three other species of wildlife classified under the Endangered Species Act: bald eagles, grizzly bears, and peregrine falcons.
RICK McINTYRE

A Forest Service fire lookout, left, uses a fire finder to chart the location of smoke sighted after a summer thunderstorm. In the 1920s and 1930s, fire towers were built throughout northwest Montana. When any smoke was spotted, the lookout transmitted the location to the nearest ranger station, and firefighters would be dispatched to the scene. LEE KAISER

ONE OF NATURE'S CROWN JEWELS

In the center of a three-piece chain of wild jewels in northwest Montana lies the magnificent mountain landscape of the Bob Marshall Wilderness. "The Bob," as it's sometimes called, is bordered to the north by the Great Bear Wilderness and to the south by the Scapegoat Wilderness. Approximately 70 percent of the the Bob Marshall's one million acres fall within the Flathead National Forest, while the rest is administered by the Lewis and Clark National Forest to the east.

Each year, thousands of hikers and horsemen travel from around the world to marvel at the grandeur of the Bob Marshall. Along the extreme eastern edge of the forest is the famous Chinese Wall—a stunning, twelve-mile-long limestone escarpment hugging the east side of the Continental Divide on the common boundary with the Lewis and Clark National Forest. The crown of this precipice soars a full one thousand feet above rich meadows, many of which provide stages for the annual mating ruts of the renowned Sun River elk herd. The wilderness also contains the icy headwaters of both the Middle and South forks of the Flathead River, the high peaks of the Flathead Alps, and the glassy, haunting waters of Big Salmon Lake.

The area takes its name from wilderness visionary Bob Marshall, who was among those responsible for the wilderness system so many Americans enjoy today. While working in the late 1930s as head of the Forest Service's Division of Recreation and Lands, Marshall implemented a ground-breaking Wilderness and Wild Area land classification system. The system ultimately was used to preserve more than fourteen million acres of western lands. Marshall also helped found the Wilderness Society, which was a key player in the passage of the National Wilderness Preservation Act of 1964.

Wilderness, wrote Marshall in the 1930s, "is vast panoramas, full of height and depth and glowing color, on a scale so overwhelming as to wipe out the ordinary meaning of dimensions. It is the song of the hermit thrush at twilight and the lapping of waves against the shoreline and the

The magnificent Chinese Wall has long been a favorite destination for travelers in the Bob Marshall Wilderness complex. This thousand-foot-high limestone escarpment forms the boundary between the Flathead and Lewis and Clark national forests. It winds for more than twelve miles through the backcountry, making it one of the most significant geological features in the northern Rockies. DAVID MUENCH

melody of wind in the trees. It is the unique odor of balsams and of freshly turned humus and of mist rising from mountain meadows. It is the feel of spruce needles under foot and sunshine on your face and wind blowing through your hair."

And it is every magnificent acre of the national forest lands that now bear his name.

Plenty of easy family afternoon trips can also be had. The Big Mountain Ski Area runs a chairlift throughout the summer months, carrying hikers to several loop trails ranging from 2.3 to 5.6 miles in length. One of these routes, the Danny On Trail, can be followed with an interpretive brochure that corresponds to numbered posts along the path, providing walkers with insights into the flora, fauna, and geology of the region. From high, windswept perches along the Danny On, hikers can take in sweeping views of Glacier National Park, the Flathead Range in the Great Bear Wilderness, the lovely Swan Range, and the myriad of shimmering lakes, streams, and rivers cradled in the valley bottoms far to the south.

First-time visitors can perhaps best wet their appetites for the Flathead National Forest in the Jewel Basin Hiking Area, approximately fifteen miles east of Kalispell. This region is open to foot traffic only and has trails appropriate for virtually any age group, including families with young children. Nearly three dozen exquisite lakes lie within the rocky folds of Jewel Basin, whose trailside vistas can cause the most jaded of mountain walkers to gasp with delight. Particularly scenic are the climb to Mt. Aeneas, as well

The graceful white-tailed deer is a common resident in lower elevation woodlands of the Flathead National Forest. This animal's senses of smell, hearing, and eyesight are all keen, allowing it to to detect the presence of any intruder. When disturbed, the whitetail will bound quickly away, its tail held upright like a flag waving through the forest. DAVE McGEE

as the trails to and past the Picnic Lakes.

Recreationists can also enjoy the 219 miles of Wild and Scenic rivers in the national forest. These federally protected waterways include the North, Middle, and South forks of the Flathead River. Within these three river systems, floaters can find everything from sleepy summer drifts on the meanders of the North Fork to a challenging float at Spruce Park on the boulder-strewn Middle Fork, which is often referred to as Montana's wildest river. Rafters, kayakers, and canoeists also may spot wildlife ranging from moose to blue heron along the rivers' shores. Each year, river outfitters on the Flathead introduce nearly sixteen thousand people to the beauties of the lower portion of the Middle Fork alone. Another three thousand people float it on their own. The national forest currently is working on several land exchanges to establish more inclusive protective corridors along these rivers.

Recreation opportunities abound in any season here. Boaters enjoy Hungry Horse Reservoir, and mountain bikers cycle the Elk Mountain National Recreation Trail. Snowmobilers zip over the mountainous paths of Marias Pass on the border of Glacier National Park, while cross-country skiers traverse trails at Round Meadow and Lion Lake.

The popularity of the Flathead National Forest has carried a price, however. In a single four-month period at Holland Lake trailhead, more than ten thousand horses, mules, and people go in or out of the Bob Marshall Wilderness. During a wet hunting season, many of the pathways turn into wide, muddy quagmires that will be scarred for years to come. The

It's safe to say that Flathead National Forest boasts some of the best whitewater rafting in Montana. Tens of thousands of people come here each year to run the three forks and the main trunk of the Flathead River, top.
MICHAEL S. SAMPLE

The brilliant, nodding head of the glacier lily, right, greets visitors to the Flathead's forests and subalpine meadows.
MICHAEL S. SAMPLE

national forest receives volunteer help from the Backcountry Horsemen of America, Student Conservation Association, and the American Hiking Society in maintaining trails. But if current use levels and backcountry maintenance budgets remain steady in the years ahead, Flathead National Forest officials estimate it may take more than fifty years to shape up the trails.

With the ballooning numbers of recreationists, Flathead National Forest officials also face the task of managing the land in a way that offers the widest spectrum of opportunities possible. Not all types of recreation are compatible. The hundred or so miles of snowmobile trails on the Flathead have been laid out separate from routes used by cross-country skiers. More and more backpackers desire footpaths free of horse use. Wilderness areas are off limits to mountain bikes, prompting calls for more access to roadways closed to motorized vehicles. The rapid increase in the use of recreation vehicles, which were virtually unheard of thirty years ago, has made it necessary to completely redesign many of the more popular campgrounds to accommodate large motorhomes.

The Flathead, with its rich ecosystems, also attracts students of all ages. One non-profit organization — the Glacier Institute — has dedicated itself to the study of the splendid natural and cultural resources in and around Glacier National Park. In 1988, the institute

Early autumn means sparring time for these big bull moose. Dominant male moose mark territories using a special scent gland and then use their formidable antlers to defend it. On rare occasions, a particularly ferocious fight can lead to two males permanently locking their antlers, resulting in death for both animals. JEFFREY T. HOGAN

obtained a special permit from Flathead National Forest to convert the former Big Creek Ranger Station into an outdoor education facility. The complex is located twenty miles north of Columbia Falls on the North Fork of the Flathead River, and its buildings have been recommended for inclusion on the National Register of Historic Places. Catering to groups desiring a residential educational experience, Big Creek Outdoor Education Center has hosted such activities as school classes, Elderhostels, and teacher workshops. Area fifth- and sixth-graders can take "hands-on" courses in earth and life sciences at Big Creek, with Flathead National Forest and Glacier National Park serving as their laboratory.

It would be hard to imagine either the intrepid adventurer or the quiet observer of nature feeling more at home anywhere in Montana than on the Flathead National Forest. This national forest overflows with beauty — from wild, frothing rivers to breathtaking mountains, from abundant big game to rich forests thick with huckleberries, wild strawberries, and wildflowers. With the national forest surrounded by so much other wild land, one has the sense on much of the Flathead that nature is somehow more boundless and more unshakable here. In these modern times, such a sensation is welcome, indeed. ■

Sixth graders and their teacher study the inner workings of a decaying stump at the Big Creek Outdoor Education Center on the Flathead National Forest, top left. MICHAEL JAVORKA

Snowmobilers travel past Great Northern Mountain, top right. The Flathead currently boasts more than one hundred miles of marked and groomed snowmobile trails. WAYNE MUMFORD

A pack train travels past autumn foliage in the Bob Marshall Wilderness, Flathead National Forest. The "Bob," as it is commonly called, welcomes an influx of hunters every fall. DIANE ENSIGN

Numerous lakes on the Flathead National Forest attract ice fishermen in the winter. These hardy anglers brave cold temperatures for the reward of tasty trout and perch — and the beauty of glorious sunrises. WAYNE MUMFORD

FLATHEAD
NATIONAL FOREST DIRECTORY

POINTS OF INTEREST

FLATHEAD WILD AND SCENIC RIVER designation covers more than two hundred miles of the South, Middle, and North forks of the Flathead River. Excellent rafting, kayaking, canoeing, bird watching, hiking, and cross-country skiing along these river corridors.

JEWEL BASIN HIKING AREA is a stunning 15,349-acre slice of high forest and mountains, lakes, streams, and wildflowers. Open to foot travel only.

HUNGRY HORSE RESERVOIR is a 34-mile reservoir tucked between the Flathead and Swan ranges, with a visitor center, campgrounds, beach areas, and boat ramps, as well as easy access into the Jewel Basin Hiking Area to the west. Fishing.

WILDERNESS AREAS

BOB MARSHALL WILDERNESS COMPLEX Contains three contiguous wilderness areas: the Bob Marshall, the Great Bear, and the Scapegoat. Approximately two-thirds of these wilderness lands are managed by the Flathead National Forest, which maintains more than one thousand miles of trails that offer the hiker and horseback rider virtually every kind of mountain experience imaginable. Use is particularly heavy during hunting season.

MISSION MOUNTAINS 73,877 acres of rugged, rocky lands, best approached from the Swan Valley to the east. Contains forty-five miles of trails, with the vast majority more suited to travel by foot than by horse.

RECREATIONAL OPPORTUNITIES

HIKING AND RIDING More than two thousand miles of trails provide a tremendous number of opportunities. More than half the trails are in wilderness areas.

CAMPING Twenty-four campgrounds, offering more than three hundred sites. (Nearly half of these are located along the shores of Hungry Horse Reservoir.) Some campgrounds remain open after Labor Day, with no water or services. Dispersed camping allowed throughout much of the forest.

SCENIC DRIVES A 115-mile loop of Forest Service roads circles Hungry Horse Reservoir, offering fine views of the Flathead and Swan ranges, as well as access to many campgrounds, beach areas, and trailheads.

RAFTING, KAYAKING AND CANOEING Fine flatwater boating on Hungry Horse Reservoir, and Holland, Tally, Van, and Swan lakes. Superb rafting, kayaking, and some canoeing on the three forks of the Flathead River. All forks of the Flathead have dangerous rapids and log jams during high water.

HUNTING Elk and white-tailed deer are plentiful. Hunting seasons also open on black bear, moose, mule deer, grizzly bear, mountain goat, and various upland birds.

FISHING Fine bull trout fishing on Flathead and Swan lakes, as well as on Hungry Horse Reservoir. Cutthroat and rainbow trout in many Flathead streams and rivers.

ALPINE SKIING The Big Mountain (six chair lifts, one T-bar, and one platter lift) is one of Montana's premier destination ski resorts.

CROSS-COUNTRY SKIING Excellent opportunities, particularly at Round Meadow, Glacier View/Cedar Trail, Lion Lake, and Essex Trail complexes, and at Blacktail Mountain.

SNOWMOBILING Popular trails include Crane Yew, fourteen miles southeast of Big Fork (37 miles occasionally groomed), Canyon Creek, 4.5 miles north of Columbia Falls (73 miles groomed), Skyline Road, one mile west of Marias Pass (39.5 miles groomed), Emery Creek, five miles east of Martin City (30 miles groomed), and 53 miles groomed in the Olney area.

OFF-ROAD VEHICLES Terrain, soils, and road/trail system are generally not suitable for trail bikes or four-wheel-drive vehicles. More than four thousand miles of road and most trails outside of wilderness areas are open to mountain bikes.

ADMINISTRATIVE OFFICES

FOREST HEADQUARTERS 1935 Third Ave. E., Kalispell, MT 59901 (406) 755-5401

HUNGRY HORSE RANGER DISTRICT P.O. Box 340, Hungry Horse, MT 59919 (406) 387-5243

GLACIER VIEW RANGER DISTRICT P.O. Box W, Columbia Falls, MT 59912 (406) 892-4372

TALLY LAKE RANGER DISTRICT 1335 Highway 93 West, Whitefish, MT 59937 (406) 862-2508

SPOTTED BEAR RANGER DISTRICT P.O. Box 310, Hungry Horse, MT 59919 (406) 752-7345

SWAN LAKE RANGER DISTRICT P.O. Box 370, Bigfork, MT 59911 (406) 837-5081

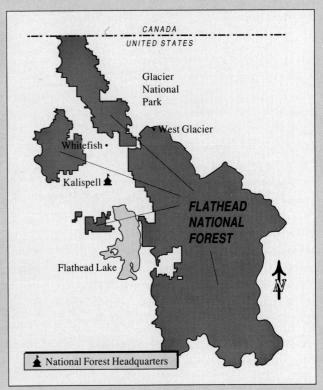

A spring-fed stream begins its long journey to the Pacific Ocean from the remote high country of the Scapegoat Wilderness in the Lolo National Forest. DAVID MUENCH

Lolo

Where history joins hands with nature

Cradled between the west slope of the Continental Divide and the sheer, granite crest of the Bitterroot Mountains in western Montana, the Lolo National Forest offers an almost endless variety of natural beauty, history, and recreation. The Lolo's more than two million acres hold enough tantalizing nooks and crannies to keep even the most ardent explorer busy for months. The automobile traveler can watch bighorn sheep along Montana Highway 200 east of Thompson Falls or roll up the magnificent Lolo Scenic Highway, climbing westward out of the Bitterroot Valley along the route made famous by Lewis and Clark. Canoeists and anglers can follow the bold, bright waters of the Bitterroot, Clearwater, Blackfoot, and Clark Fork rivers. Hikers can fan out into the wilds of the Rattlesnake, Scapegoat, and Welcome Creek wilderness areas or the Blue Mountain and Pattee Canyon recreation areas.

Western Montana's largest population center, Missoula, is surrounded by this national forest. But a kind of gentle integration exists between the city and the Lolo National Forest that would be the envy of any urban planner. Literally minutes from downtown Missoula, hikers can walk the trails of the 33,000-acre Rattlesnake Wilderness, pull trout from the Clark Fork River, slide a canoe into the Bitterroot River from a fine new launching ramp, or simply lounge beneath the tall, cool pines of a Pattee Canyon campground.

The lay of the land and the movement of weather patterns across the mountains of the Lolo have created patchwork quilts of vegetation. Stands of ponderosa pine, Douglas-fir, lodgepole pine, and — on the cool slopes of the high mountains — subalpine fir and western larch cover Lolo National Forest. The widely varying mosaic of timber on the Lolo not only provides commercial timber, but also essential habitat for a wide range of wildlife species.

Indeed, in the Lolo — as in every national forest in Montana — wildlife is an important resource. The Lolo contains 3,500 miles of trout fisheries and 350,000 acres of elk winter range. It also is home to moose, deer, bighorn sheep, Rocky Mountain goat, fishers, bald eagles, osprey by the dozens, peregrine falcons, boreal owls, harlequin ducks, and — of all things — an occasional family or two of loons bobbing on the waters of Seeley Lake.

Lolo National Forest managers and local citizens have made a strong commitment to preserving this bounty of wildlife, giving wildlife management top priority in a number of areas on the Lolo. The national

Unlike other conifers, the needles of the western larch, below and bottom, turn gold in autumn and drop off. Larch can grow to tremendous sizes, sometimes reaching heights of two hundred feet. Regional Indian peoples had high regard for the tree's sweet sap, which they gathered by carving cavities in the trunks of certain trees. MICHAEL S. SAMPLE (both)

forest also manages the vast majority of its trout streams to maintain strong populations of native fish, such as the west-slope cutthroat trout and bull trout. Rock Creek, located just thirty minutes from downtown Missoula, is after several decades still considered one of the best trout streams in western Montana.

Forest visitors can drink in the sheer beauty of this country by foot, ski, canoe, or even hang glider off Mt. Sentinel, as well as rub elbows with history here. The old Ninemile Remount Depot, for example, offers an interesting side trip. It's the only pack stock remount depot ever built by the Forest Service and the spot where early smokejumpers drifted from the sky half a century ago. The visitor center of the Aerial Fire Depot at Missoula County Airport also is a must for those interested in smokejumping. The center is open from May 30 to September 15. Many old homesteader

buildings also are scattered throughout the Lolo, including the Hogback Cabin along the beautiful upper stretches of Rock Creek. Skiers, snowshoers, and snowmobilers can rent some old and restored structures, such as the West Fork Butte fire lookout and the Clearwater Crossing and Driveway Peak cabins, during the winter months.

The Lolo also contains the old Savenac Nursery, where tremendous numbers of white pine, ponderosa, and western larch seedlings once were grown and then sent for planting throughout the forests of the Northwest. Three million seedlings were produced at Savenac each year during the 1920s. By the 1930s, that number had swelled to twelve million trees annually. Most of the nursery's buildings near Haugen are still standing. Although the buildings are closed to the public, visitors can drive through the nursery complex.

The Lolo offers so much to do and see that visitors

An early training center for smokejumpers opened on the Lolo National Forest in 1941. Today, about four hundred smokejumpers are employed each year on national forests throughout the country. Many receive their training at the Aerial Fire Depot, just outside of Missoula.
WAYNE WILLIAMS

Elk hunters use llamas to pack into a remote region of the Lolo National Forest, right. More than thirteen thousand elk live on the Lolo, including one of the finest bull populations in the state. JAN WASSINK

Before the days of smokejumpers, equipment needed to fight forest fires was carried by teams of mules and horses. The Ninemile Remount Center served as a provision center for these animals.
GEOFFREY SUTTON (all photos)

AN EARLY ERA OF FIREFIGHTING

An engaging slice of history can be found in the lovely Ninemile Creek Valley, just twenty-five miles west of Missoula. This area contains the Ninemile Remount Depot, which for more than twenty years provided the main link for packing supplies by mule to firefighters battling blazes in the rugged mountains of Idaho, Wyoming, and Montana.

In the first decades of the twentieth century, the rangers of the newly established Forest Service found themselves with the overwhelming task of protecting millions of acres of timber land from the ravages of fire. They usually had nothing more than an axe and shovel to fight blazes that often burned in extremely inaccessible territory, cut only by a thin braid of game paths and old prospectors' trails. Then came the long, hot summer of 1910. By August, a series of small lightning fires grew together and raged across western Montana and northern Idaho, ultimately scorching nearly 3 million acres of timber and killing more than eighty people. It was one of the worst fire seasons in recorded history. The Forest Service swung into action the following year, constructing a major network of trails to provide better access to the region. It also ran telephone lines to the tops of high mountains and hired lookouts, who then called rangers with the location of any fire they spotted.

Until the arrival of smokejumpers in the 1940s and 1950s, horses and mules carried all fire equipment into the mountains, including the heavy plows used to cut fire lines. For a time, the Forest Service rented the large numbers of needed stock animals from area ranchers, at a rate of fifty cents per day per animal. The arrangement worked fine until the 1920s, when most ranchers started selling off their horsepower for mechanical tractors and threshers. During the severe

fire season of 1929, commercial stock simply ran out, forcing the Forest Service into the livestock business.

The "remount" concept was borrowed from the United States Army, which set up such depots to obtain, train, and issue horses to cavalry troops. So in the valley of Ninemile Creek in 1932 rose the first and only Forest Service Remount Depot. Over the next several decades, the center supplied stock for fire crews throughout the region and perfected the tricky job of packing mules and horses.

Today, the Remount Depot is in a stage of rebirth. The original buildings have been meticulously restored, and a fine new visitor center highlights the fanciful history of the remount operations. The Ninemile Wildlands Training Center is also located here. This educational facility teaches Forest Service personnel from around the country the proper use of wilderness and offers some of the best courses in the West on packing, the construction and maintenance of trails, and the preservation of historic structures. The grounds also continue to be an important wintering area for Forest Service livestock.

may find a challenge in simply deciding where to start. The national forest provides access to four wilderness areas, with the Rattlesnake and Welcome Creek wildernesses close to Missoula. The Lolo also contains portions of the Scapegoat Wilderness in westcentral Montana and the Selway-Bitterroot Wilderness, an area shared by Montana and Idaho.

Outdoor lovers visiting Missoula should hike into the Rattlesnake National Recreation Area. This 59,000-acre area, barely a stone's throw from the city of Missoula, contains numerous mountain nooks and streamside crannies that insulate hikers from the outside world — including 33,000 acres of congressionally designated wilderness. Because of high use in the Rattlesnake, camping is prohibited within three miles of the main entrances, including the Sawmill Gulch and Woods Gulch trailheads. But beyond those three easy miles, the area is open to use by

The western tanager, above, is one of the loveliest of all the Lolo's feathered residents. These birds spend most of their time high in the canopies of coniferous forests, although they occasionally can be seen as they swoop down to to feed on berries and insects. JAN WASSINK

Catching a glimpse of the secretive bobcat, left, is a highlight for any nature lover. Feeding primarily on small rodents and an occasional upland game bird, this beautiful animal will sometimes drop on unsuspecting prey from an overhanging tree limb. JESS R. LEE

backpackers, who might see black bear, elk, deer, moose, and even mountain goats.

Also located just minutes from downtown Missoula is the 5,500-acre Blue Mountain recreation area, a beautiful mix of meadow and mountain crossed by a fine network of forest roads and trails frequented by mountain bikers, off-highway vehicle users, hikers, and snowmobilers. A short, wheelchair-accessible nature trail just a few miles from the entrance leads to a sprawling view of the Missoula Valley. Another nature trail and canoe portage complex along the Bitterroot River is located nearby and is open to wheelchair use. The extremely rich bottomland ecosystem here is awash with wildlife ranging from deer to pheasants to nesting ducks. Moore Lake, located in the wild, timbered country along the Montana-Idaho border, has facilities for the disabled and a trail to the lake that is accessible by wheelchair.

To the northeast of Missoula lies the fabulous Seeley Lake Ranger District — a wild tapestry of trees, mountains, streams, and glacial lakes. No fewer than five spectacular loop roads allow visitors to view the region by car. Good drives for first-time visitors include the fourteen-mile Clearwater Loop, with its sweeping views of the Swan Range, and the seventeen-mile Richmond Ridge Road, with vistas of the Mission and Swan mountains and the Clearwater and Swan valleys. Those itching to escape the confines of the car should don a pair of walking shoes and set out on the Morrell Falls National Recreation Trail or the easy footpaths that lead to Bear and Colt lakes.

A float on the gentle, lovely meanders of a 3.5-mile stretch of the Clearwater River provides an especially good opportunity to soak in the beauty of the Seeley Lake region. Known as the Clearwater Canoe Trail, the float begins near Montana Highway 83 just north of the

The sun lights up the rocky flanks of Scapegoat Mountain in the Scapegoat Wilderness. Nearly 75,000 acres of the 239,000-acre wilderness lie on the Lolo National Forest. CAL RYDER

Morrell Mountain rises on the crest of the Swan Range in the Lolo National Forest. The range, which stretches northward into the Flathead National Forest, looms four to five thousand feet above the Swan Valley to the east. MICHAEL S. SAMPLE

Seeley Lake Ranger Station. After winding through country that holds deer, moose, finches, grebes, ducks, and warblers (indeed, more bird life than most people would see in an entire season), the Clearwater delivers floaters to the north end of Seeley Lake, just across from the takeout point at the Seeley Ranger Station. Those with only one vehicle can then make the easy 1.5-mile trek by trail back to the put-in point.

Cross-country skiers should note that the Seeley Lake nordic ski trail complex is located just south of the ranger station. The complex contains nearly a dozen ski trails, ranging from groomed and easy to routes that climb sharply through virtually untracked forest. Most of the area also is open to snowmobiles. Downhill skiers can head for the powder of either the Snow Bowl or Marshall ski areas, both of which are found on the Lolo National Forest near Missoula.

With its mix of rugged country, shimmering lakes, recreation opportunities, and historic features, the Lolo truly holds something for all who visit it. ∎

Elk gather in the soft white flakes of an autumn snowstorm. In early fall, travelers through Lolo's backcountry may hear the sound of male elk bugling — a high-pitched whistle that often brings two bulls together for a sparring match. DENVER A. BRYAN

THE LOONS OF SEELEY LAKE

Writing of how he loved to lie awake at night and listen to the sounds of woodland creatures, Henry David Thoreau confessed in The Maine Woods: "I had listened to hear some words or syllables of their language, but it chanced that I listened in vain until I heard the cry of the loon." People don't normally think of the West as a place to see or hear this spectacular bird. But about thirty nesting pairs inhabit Montana's 145,000 square miles. Most can be found in an area bounded by Helena on the east and south, the Idaho border on the west, and the Canadian border on the north. Within this region, visitors often can spot loons in two areas of the national forest system. One of those is on the Kootenai National Forest at Murphy Lake. The other is on the Lolo National Forest, at a beautiful spot called Seeley Lake.

While adult loons have relatively few natural predators, they are extremely sensitive to encroachment by man. Hunters no longer use loons for target practice, as was fairly common a half-century ago. But the proliferation of lakeside cottages, acid rain, and in some parts of the country, mercury poisoning, have taken massive tolls on these enchanting birds. (Canoeists or hikers at Seeley Lake who spot loons should always give them a wide berth.)

The loons of Seeley Lake are thought to winter on the Gulf of Mexico, leaving sometime in April for the long trip to northwest Montana. Little is known about their exact migration route. Most researchers suspect the birds fly up through the panhandle of Texas, follow a corridor over eastern Colorado and Wyoming, and finally head west once they reach the southeastern corner of Montana. The late springs in this region often force the Seeley Lake loons to mate and nest when snow is still on the ground, to ensure that their chicks will be strong enough to fly south the following autumn.

The female loon typically lays two eggs, and both she and the male will take turns incubating the eggs for twenty-five to thirty days, until they hatch. Though chicks enter the water soon after birth, they spend most of their first two weeks on their parents' backs. It will be fully three months before they can catch fish on their own.

Loons are not the premier attraction of Lolo National Forest. Indeed, most people don't know they even exist here. Yet walking through the pines on the shore of Seeley Lake some starlit summer night and suddenly hearing the loon's clear, haunting call provides visitors with a delightfully different national forest experience.

The name is "common loon," but loons are anything but common in Montana. Two lakes in Montana national forests — Murphy in the Kootenai and Seeley in the Lolo — provide nesting areas for this striking symbol of wild areas.
DANIEL J. COX

LOLO
NATIONAL FOREST DIRECTORY

POINTS OF INTEREST

RATTLESNAKE NATIONAL RECREATION AREA is located four miles north of Missoula. It's marked by sheer, narrow valleys with Douglas-fir, lodgepole pine, and larch, along with glacial basins, eighteen lakes, and nearly a dozen major streams. Contains the 33,000-acre Rattlesnake Wilderness.

NINEMILE VISITOR CENTER is a historic mule/horse remount center used extensively for fighting wildfires in Montana, Idaho, and Wyoming during the 1930s and 1940s. Located northwest of Missoula.

AERIAL FIRE DEPOT AND SMOKEJUMPER CENTER at the Missoula County Airport, northwest of Missoula. Excellent visitor center with a reconstructed fire lookout tower, historical photos, and pictorial dioramas.

WILDERNESS AREAS

RATTLESNAKE 33,000 acres containing high lakes, cirque basins, and steep canyons. Located seven miles from Missoula, with easy access from the east, south, and west.

SCAPEGOAT 74,192 acres located on the Lolo. Beautiful streams, alpine meadows and dramatic limestone escarpments. Can be reached on forest roads off of Montana Highway 200.

SELWAY-BITTERROOT 9,767 acres located on the Lolo, reachable on forest roads west off of U.S. Highway 93. Lolo lands make up only a small portion of the wilderness, but excellent hiking is found along the South Fork of Lolo Creek and on a two-day round-trip to 9,069-foot Lolo Peak.

WELCOME CREEK 28,135 acres of steep forested ridges and narrow canyons, located approximately twenty miles southeast of Missoula.

RECREATIONAL OPPORTUNITIES

HIKING AND RIDING More than 1,800 miles of trails open to foot and horseback travel. Eight National Recreation Trails, including the Pattee Canyon Ski Touring Trail five miles southeast of Missoula and the Blue Mountain Equestrian Trail three miles southwest of Missoula.

CAMPING Twenty-seven campgrounds, with the biggest concentration located along Rock Creek Road, Swan Forest Highway, and Interstate 90. Dispersed camping allowed in most of the forest.

RECREATIONAL CABINS Clearwater Crossing Cabin in the Ninemile Ranger District, Driveway Peak Cabin in the Plains-Thompson Falls Ranger District, and West Fork Butte Lookout in the Missoula Ranger District. For more information, contact individual forest district offices.

KAYAKING, RAFTING AND CANOEING Clark Fork River has few rapids, but diversion dams and fences require close attention. Portions of Rock Creek are usually floatable by raft until the beginning of July. The Seeley Lake Ranger District contains the beautiful Clearwater Canoe Trail, with the launch site located two miles north of the Seeley Lake Ranger Station.

HUNTING Fine elk herds. Hunting seasons also open for mountain goat, bighorn sheep, deer, black bear, and various game birds.

FISHING More than 3,500 miles of fishing streams, including the famed Rock Creek trout stream. Nearly one hundred lakes. Cutthroat, rainbow, brook, and bull trout are common.

ALPINE SKIING Montana Snow Bowl, twelve miles northeast of Missoula (two chair lifts, one T-bar, and one rope tow) and Marshall Ski Area, seven miles north of Missoula (one chair lift, one T-bar, and two rope tows).

CROSS-COUNTRY SKIING 150 miles of marked cross-country trails scattered throughout the forest, with popular trails at Pattee Canyon, Seeley Lake, and Lolo Pass.

SLEDDING Sled and tubing hill at Blue Mountain recreation area, southwest of Missoula.

SNOWMOBILING Popular areas with marked and groomed trails include the Seeley Lake East Side System (65 miles of trail), Lolo Creek System west of Lolo (108 miles of trail), and Blue Mountain southwest of Missoula (14 miles of trail). Several Snow Play areas accessible from Lolo Pass Winter Sports Area.

OFF-ROAD VEHICLES Trails for mountain bikes, trail bikes, four-wheel-drive vehicles and off-road vehicles at Blue Mountain recreation area. For more information, contact the Missoula Ranger District.

ADMINISTRATIVE OFFICES

FOREST HEADQUARTERS Building 24, Fort Missoula, Missoula, MT 59801 (406) 329-3750

MISSOULA RANGER DISTRICT Building 24-A, Fort Missoula, MT 59801 (406) 329-3750

PLAINS/THOMPSON FALLS RANGER DISTRICT P.O. Box 429, Plains, MT 59859 (406) 826-3821

SUPERIOR RANGER DISTRICT Superior, MT 59872 (406) 822-4233

NINEMILE RANGER DISTRICT Huson, MT 59846 (406) 626-5201

SEELEY LAKE RANGER DISTRICT Box 717, Seeley Lake, MT 59868 (406) 677-2233

A wind-shorn, subalpine landscape leads to the foot of El Capitan, a 9,983-foot sentinel in the Selway-Bitterroot Wilderness. The wilderness stretches from just west of Montana's Bitterroot Valley to nearly the center of Idaho. MICHAEL S. SAMPLE

Bitterroot

A spectacular mountain retreat

According to Flathead Indian legend, the bitterroot flower, from which this national forest takes its name, was created when one morning at dawn, the rising sun found an old woman weeping by the river for her starving people. The sun took pity on her and sent a beautiful guardian bird to comfort her. "Your tears will cause a new plant to rise," said the bird. "The flower will have the white color of your hair and the rose of my wing feathers. Though you'll find the root bitter from your sorrow, it will nourish you." And nourish it did. For both the Flathead and Kootenai Indians, the bitterroot formed the most important root harvest of any plant in western Montana.

The bitterroot plant actually was named by Lewis and Clark in 1805. Since that time it has been selected as Montana's state flower, and its name has been bestowed on a variety of natural features along the west side of the Continental Divide. Wrote one observer in 1898: "A beautiful flower, a beautiful river, a valley, a magnificent range — such is the Bitter Root." Had that writer waited another eight years, to the time when the Bitterroot National Forest was established, he most certainly could have added that to his list of praiseworthy features.

The Bitterroot National Forest contains more than 1.6 million acres that drift eastward from the Idaho panhandle over the fiercely rugged Bitterroot Mountains, the east-west drainages sliced open into rugged valleys by the likes of Tin Cup, Lost Horse, and Roaring Lion creeks. This is powerful, dramatic country. The peaks on the eastern flanks of the Bitterroot Mountains rise more than five thousand feet in three miles. After leaving this range, the national forest continues on the other side of the Bitterroot Valley, rolling across the somewhat more subdued, though hardly less enticing, Sapphire Mountains.

The Bitterroot can keep outdoor enthusiasts busy for months. The national forest has more than 650 miles of trails open to mountain bikes and off-highway vehicle use. Another 950 miles of trail provide foot and horse access to nearly 750,000 acres of congressionally protected wild lands, including portions of the Selway-Bitterroot, Anaconda-Pintler, and Idaho's Frank Church-River of No Return wilderness areas. The Continental Divide National Scenic Trail in the southeastern portion of the national forest offers striking views into the Big Hole Valley and the Anaconda-Pintler Wilderness. Also noteworthy are the Lake Como Loop and Palisade Mountain national recreation trails, as well as the five-mile trek to the 150-foot Overwhich Falls. Those with cars or small trucks may want to negotiate eight rather bumpy miles of gravel road from U.S. Highway 93 near Hamilton to Lost Horse Observation Point — a spectacular perch from which to bask in long, lovely views of the

---

From the top of Trapper Peak in the Selway-Bitterroot Wilderness, the world falls away in an endless cascade of rocky ridgelines. More than 500,000 acres of this 1.3 million-acre wilderness are located on the Bitterroot National Forest. DAVID MUENCH

Bitterroot Range to the west.

The Bitterroot also contains an abundance of walking and driving routes with great historical significance. For example, a system of trails and roadways has preserved much of Lewis and Clark's original route to the Pacific Ocean. Likewise, visitors can follow in the footsteps of the Reverend Samuel Parker, thought to be the first white man to travel the South Nez Perce Indian Trail in 1835. Chief Joseph and the Nez Perce also crossed the Bitterroot as they fled from federal troops in 1877.

Today, people from all over North America come to the Bitterroot seeking its high peaks, which are certainly as spectacular as any in the state. Yet visitors also can relish the national forest's beauty simply by roaming through the wide variety of vegetation that covers these lands. The drier valley floor and lower foothills of the Bitterroot Valley hold an arid-lands mix of sage, juniper, and paintbrush, broken in places by stately stands of ponderosa pine. Higher up, the land receives more moisture and is thus richer. Within thirty minutes from the semi-arid, 3,000-foot high Bitterroot Valley, hikers can pass through fine stands of grand fir, Douglas-fir, and western larch and note river birch and alder along the stream bottoms. The forest floor also grows lusher, much of it carpeted with kinnikinnick, pinegrass, huckleberry, beargrass, and snowberry. And in the upper elevations stand spruce and subalpine fir, with their dark green branches framing pockets of lush meadow.

The Indians once relied heavily on the region's ponderosa pine, as can be seen at the Indian Trees Campground south of Darby. The scars visible on several of the large ponderosas here stem from the days

Wild strawberries, above, peek through the underbrush, a tempting taste treat for passersby and wildlife alike.
MICHAEL S. SAMPLE

More than one thousand miles of maintained roads await visitors to the Bitterroot National Forest. This one, right, cradled by the shimmering golden branches of western larch trees, runs through the bottom of Bear Creek Canyon. MICHAEL S. SAMPLE

PIONEERS OF THE FOREST SERVICE

"We didn't receive instructions about anything much," confessed early forest ranger Than Wilkerson, "so we did about as we pleased." And thus at Hughes Creek on the Bitterroot National Forest, it "pleased" Wilkerson and his co-worker to construct the Alta Ranger Station, one of the first ranger stations in America. "We built the cabin on our own initiative," Wilkerson went on to explain. "We paid for the nails, the hinges, for the door that we made, the four-paned window, and the U.S. flag we put on the tip of a 20-foot lodgepole to float over our cabin on the Fourth of July, 1899."

The cabin was manned by Wilkerson and Henry Tuttle for five years. Then a mini-gold rush to Hughes Creek pushed the land into private ownership. But in 1941, the Hamilton Lion's Club purchased the original site at Hughes Creek and donated it to the Forest Service. The Alta Ranger station is located thirty-three miles south of Conner, on State Road 473.

The conditions and terms of employment for early rangers like Wilkerson can either be described as adventurous or abominable. Just after the turn of the century, rangers were earning sixty to seventy-five dollars a month, with no reimbursement for expenses. Former Bitterroot Supervisor John Lowell tells of being sent into the field his first summer with no more than a Use Book, a marking hatchet, some pencils and writing paper, a scale rule, and a packet of free-use timber permits. The forest supervisor, he recalls, told him only to "stay away from the towns entirely during the summer periods."

After ninety years, the Alta Ranger Station still stands proudly in the piney mountains south of Conner.
GLENN VAN NIMWEGEN

when Indian women harvested the bark for the sweet layer of cambium beneath. Waiting for a cool spring day when the sap was running, Kootenai women would use a chisel made from the bone of an elk or the branch of a juniper to peel away large strips of bark from selected trees — typically on only one side of the tree, in order not to kill it. Another tool made from a sheep's horn then was used to separate the sweet cambium layer from the outer bark. This special treat would be consumed on the spot.

The upper reaches of the Bitterroot Mountains also hold the subalpine larch — a special tree found only in a few places in the United States. These trees grow in the fiercest, least hospitable environments imaginable. They hang from sheer rocks by their roots, looking like gnarled old men huddled in the face of a raging storm. Each year, aided by only the briefest, most fleeting summers, the subalpine larch produces a considerable crop of purple-scaled cones that drop to the ground as the first chill of autumn rolls across the high country. Unlike true conifers, larch do not keep their needles through the winter. Soon after the cones have dropped, the needles turn a bright gold and fall off, drifting into a thousand rocky nooks and crannies on the high crest of the timberline.

Although increased moisture at higher elevations on the Bitterroot National Forest creates some solid timber stands, the steep slopes that mark much of the

A magnificent grove of western larch, top right, reaches for the sky. Unlike other Rocky Mountain conifers, the needles of the larch turn gold and drop off with the arrival of autumn. The tree is at its best growing in cool, moist sites, but can also be found in a variety of other habitats.
MICHAEL S. SAMPLE

An inquisitive young pine marten, right, pauses on its daily errands for a closer look. This graceful, agile acrobat spends most of its time in trees looking for its favorite prey — the red squirrel.
ERWIN AND PEGGY BAUER

terrain here reduces the amount of timber available for harvest. Nevertheless, in 1988, 25.7 million board feet of commercial timber was cut on the Bitterroot, along with more than 3,082 cords of firewood and 5,660 Christmas trees.

The Bitterroot's sheer, plunging terrain also poses challenges to firefighters. In the summer of 1988, hot, dry conditions caused 135 fires to burn more than 31,000 acres of the Bitterroot National Forest (7,400 of which were in Idaho). The rugged lands tested the skill and resolve of those pitted against the blazes.

During pitched battles to control particularly inaccessible fires that year, such as those that burned on Rock Creek and Totem Peak, helicopters made trip after trip to nearby rivers and lakes to pick up water to drop on the flames. When the burns were finally over,

fire lines cut through steep terrain had to be carefully covered with tree limbs and other brush to help prevent erosion. Likewise, the immediate reseeding of young trees was of paramount importance.

Joining the Bitterroot firefighting efforts that summer were 160 students from the Trapper Creek Job Corps Center, which today is one of the brightest stars of the Bitterroot National Forest. Operated by the national forest in cooperation with the U.S. Department of Labor, the center houses young men and women and provides vocational education for them. Its offerings range from beginning reading courses to a high school diploma. The center also offers first-rate vocational instruction in carpentry, painting, electrical work, cement finishing, cooking, welding, and building maintenance. The placement rate for

No creature alive can dance up and down the sheer cliffs and and precipices of the northern Rocky Mountain high country with more ease than the mountain goat. The hoofs of these magnificent creatures are split into two toes —the bottoms of each lined with spongy traction pads that help grab hold on slippery surfaces. MICHAEL S. SAMPLE

graduates stands well above eighty percent — a success story substantial enough to have recently earned Trapper Creek the honor of being voted the top Job Corps Center in the United States.

With the exception of hunters, who come from all over the world to try for trophy elk, bighorn sheep, and mountain goat, the Bitterroot is largely an "off the beaten path" national forest — one frequented

A pika, or "rock rabbit," enjoys a summer snack of bluebells, right. While a shrill "eeeeeek, eeeeeek" may alert you that a pika is nearby, its coloring makes it very difficult to see. JEFF FOOTT

It would be hard to find a plant with a more showy flower than the bitterroot, below, which Montanans have made their state flower. The bitterroot was once an extremely important food crop for native peoples. MICHAEL S. SAMPLE

The jagged point of Prinz Ridge slices the sky above Blodgett Canyon in the Bitterroot National Forest. Much of this national forest is marked by sheer, soaring terrain, much to the delight of national forest visitors seeking incomparable scenery. MICHAEL S. SAMPLE

A SACRED SHRINE

Ten miles south of Darby, on the east side of U.S. Highway 93, stands an old ponderosa pine with a history matched by few other trees in America. The Medicine Tree, as it's now called, was first written about by fur trapper Alexander Ross, who passed by it in the spring of 1833. "Here a curiosity called the Ram's Horn—out of a large pine five feet from root projects a ram's head, the horns which are transfixed to the middle," he writes. "The natives cannot tell when this took place but tradition says when the first hunter passed this way he shot an arrow at a mountain ram and wounded him; the animal turned on his assailant who jumped behind the tree. The animal missing its aim pierced the tree with his horns and killed himself. The tree appears to have grown around the horns."

Another legend says that coyote, the trickster, posed a challenge to a ram who loved to boast about his great power. "Let's see how strong you are," suggested the coyote. "Can you knock over this young pine?" Charging with all his might, the ram caught one horn in the tree and hung there helpless, much to the

amusement of coyote. Later, a band of Salish Indians riding by cut the ram down, though the one horn remained stuck firmly in the trunk. After this, the tree became a symbol of strength to the Salish and their neighbors, the Nez Perce Indians.

Scarcely a trapper, miner, or explorer who passed the Medicine Tree failed to mention it. Most of them also noted that local Indians regularly made offerings of shells, beads, horns, tobacco, or buckskin to the tree as they passed.

Although the ram's horns have since been engulfed by the trunk of the tree, this mighty ponderosa remains a special tree to the Kootenai-Salish people. They still make offerings on a regular basis. Visitors to the Medicine Tree should treat it and any gifts placed around it with respect, making sure not to desecrate what may have been a sacred shrine for more than three hundred years.

MARK LAGERSTROM, both

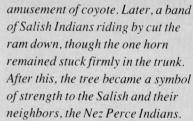

most heavily by residents of Missoula and the Bitterroot Valley. The national forest has an unhurried, "locals" kind of feel, whether recreationists are fishing for cutthroat trout along the shores of beautiful Lake Como, following old pioneer wagon ruts on the trail to the Big Hole Battlefield, or skiing through knee-deep powder at Lost Trail Pass ski area. Time has been kind to the Bitterroot. In many ways, it remains as fresh and inspiring as the day it was set aside as one of America's first forest reserves. ■

Another quiet night begins in the Selway-Bitterroot Wilderness, top. Trapper Peak is in the background, to the right of center. The West Fork, Darby, and Stevensville ranger districts of the Bitterroot National Forest contain a number of trailheads that provide access to this unforgettable slice of high country. MICHAEL S. SAMPLE

Winter cloaks Mt. Jerusalem, left, in a soft blanket of snow. Winter touring of the Bitterroot National Forest high country is becoming increasingly popular, although in some areas the steep terrain poses the danger of avalanches. MARK LAGERSTROM

BITTERROOT
NATIONAL FOREST DIRECTORY

POINTS OF INTEREST

BITTERROOT WILDFLOWER AREA offers splendid views of the Bitterroot Valley. Common wildflowers include mountain heath, rhododendron, pentstemon, fairy slipper, beargrass, columbine, glacier lily, clematis, trillium, and bitterroot. Located along an old logging road, northwest of Hamilton.

BIG HOLE BATTLEFIELD TRAIL begins on the east side of U.S. Highway 93, six miles south of the Sula Ranger Station. This is the route traveled by Chief Joseph and the Nez Perce tribe in 1877, in their epic attempt to escape capture by U.S. Cavalry troops. The trail climbs 3.8 miles to the Gibbons Pass Area. Hikers are advised to start at Hogan's Cabin on the east side of the Continental Divide, to avoid an uphill climb all the way.

SKALKAHO FALLS is located at the end of Montana Highway 38, eighteen miles east of the junction with U.S. Highway 93. This scenic mountain pass road is open only in the summer.

TRAPPER PEAK is the highest point in the Selway-Bitterroot Wilderness. The rugged 10,157-foot mountain can be viewed from a scenic pullout along U.S. Highway 93 or climbed by way of a steep trail up the back side.

WILDERNESS AREAS

SELWAY-BITTERROOT Approximately 250,000 acres of the 1.3 million-acre Selway-Bitterroot are located in the Montana portion of the Bitterroot National Forest, which spills over into Idaho. Spectacular canyons and sheer mountain slopes. Wildlife is plentiful, and trout fishing is good in most lakes and streams.

ANACONDA-PINTLER 41,162 acres located on the Bitterroot. A beautiful land of rocky glacial basins, icy streams, and high mountain lakes.

RECREATIONAL OPPORTUNITIES

HIKING AND RIDING More than 1,600 miles of trails, including five national recreation trails: Palisade Mountain (six miles), Easthouse (twenty-three miles), Lake Como Loop (seven miles), Bighole Battlefield (3.8 miles), and Continental Divide National Scenic Trail (approximately fifty miles).

CAMPING Eighteen campgrounds on the Montana portion of the Bitterroot National Forest. Dispersed camping allowed in most areas.

RECREATIONAL CABINS East Fork Guard Station on the Sula Ranger District. Open all year.

RAFTING AND KAYAKING Outstanding whitewater rafting on the Selway River in Idaho, by permit only.

ROCK CLIMBING Several good climbing areas on the Stevensville Ranger District.

HUNTING Although many species of big game live on the Bitterroot, elk hunting is especially popular. Individual ranger districts have lists of outfitters.

FISHING Fine cutthroat and rainbow trout fisheries exist in most Bitterroot lakes and streams.

ALPINE SKIING Lost Trail Powder Mountain (two lifts and two rope tows), on the Sula Ranger District ninety miles south of Missoula.

CROSS-COUNTRY SKIING Excellent in the open meadows near Lost Trail Pass.

SNOWMOBILING Several dispersed areas throughout the forest. Check with individual ranger districts for more information.

OFF-ROAD VEHICLES Portions of the more than six hundred miles of trail outside of wilderness areas are open to use by motorized vehicles and mountain bikes. Contact individual districts for more information.

ADMINISTRATIVE OFFICES

FOREST HEADQUARTERS 316 N. Third St., Hamilton, MT 59840 (406) 363-3131

DARBY RANGER DISTRICT Box 266, Darby, MT 59829 (406) 821-3913

SULA RANGER DISTRICT Sula, MT 59871 (406) 821-3201

STEVENSVILLE RANGER DISTRICT 88 Main St., Stevensville, MT 59870 (406) 777-5461

WEST FORK RANGER DISTRICT Darby, MT 59829 (406) 821-3269

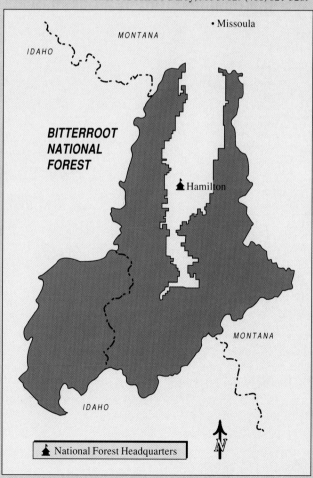

BITTERROOT NATIONAL FOREST

▲ National Forest Headquarters

The 776,000-acre Rocky Mountain Front, located on the Rocky Mountain Ranger District of the Lewis and Clark National Forest, contains some of the most spectacular scenery in western Montana. LARRY MAYER

Lewis and Clark

Lands of contrast

There's a magnificent breadth to the beauty of the Lewis and Clark National Forest, one that seems nearly as wide and unfettered as the natural features of Montana itself. Smooth, rounded mountains cradle semi-arid mosaics of windswept, grassy valleys on the eastern, or Jefferson Division, of this national forest in northcentral Montana. This land also holds the Big and Little Snowy mountains, as well as the Castle, Crazy, Little Belt, and Highwood ranges. Each of these mountain systems contains its own medley of trees, streams, and grassy meadow lands, sometimes spiced by striking limestone and sandstone cliffs and canyons.

The Rocky Mountain Division, on the other hand, lies far to the west, across a wide swath of agricultural land resting on the breast of the Great Plains. Marked by a dramatic line of folded limestone and dolomite, this region is commonly referred to as the Overthrust Belt — actually a small but dramatic slice of a larger geologic fold and thrust belt extending all the way from Alaska to Mexico. Northern Montana is truly magnificent here. Sprawled over 750,000 acres south of Glacier National Park are glacier-scoured headlands, hanging valleys, and rocky cirque basins — a land revered by the thousands of visitors who explore it every year. In July, they can look up from Halfmoon Park and watch mountain goats perform dizzy pirouettes on the sheer flanks of Scapegoat Mountain. In autumn, the air resounds with the sharp

These dramatic, plunging precipices high above the Sun River at Castle Reef are part of the Overthrust Belt, a massive fold and thrust belt that extends from Alaska all the way to Mexico. BYRON BONNEY

ring of bugling elk. And in the spring, grizzly bear wander the hillsides, searching for carcasses of elk and mule deer brought down by the harsh elements of winter.

Many of the same geological processes that formed the magnificent mountains of the Rocky Mountain Division also left extremely rich deposits of oil and gas in the region. Geologists believe the Montana Overthrust Belt may hide more than 600 million barrels of oil and nearly 10 trillion cubic feet of natural gas. Most of these reserves are thought to lie beneath the Lewis and Clark National Forest. It comes as no surprise, then, that oil and gas leases have been issued on more than 85 percent of the non-wilderness lands of Lewis and Clark's Rocky Mountain Division.

Such resource potential may make the hearts of oil men soar, but it also brings a lump to the throats of many who want to protect the integrity of this fragile, stunning ecosystem. A report by the Forest Service notes concerns about the effects development, and any accompanying road-building, may have on the streams and soils of the Rocky Mountain Front.

Thus the stage has been set for yet another classic showdown between those who favor maintaining national forest lands primarily for recreation and wildlife protection and those who favor the extraction of natural resources. Recreation-based businesses such as outfitter services, restaurants, and motels currently provide three times as many jobs in this area as do resource-based businesses. Some people in the tourism-related industries fear those jobs might be compromised by large-scale extraction of any mineral or petroleum product — activities that would create different types of jobs.

Management of the Lewis and Clark National Forest wasn't always so complicated. The forest rangers of the early 1900s found life, if not easy, at least fairly straight-forward. To land a job in a national forest, one early forest ranger said, men were required to be "thoroughly sound and able bodied, capable of enduring hardships and of performing severe labor under trying conditions." Those who passed the required tests — such as shooting, packing, and horsemanship — were sent off to patrol for fires, chase the occasional poacher, issue timber permits, and build guard stations, fire towers, and living quarters. Their salary came to $720 a year, horse and saddle not included. "The Forest Service was a new thing," recalls longtime Forest Service ranger Clyde Fickes of his early days in the Sun River country. "You had to sell people on the concept. You fraternized with your neighbors and you tried to help out."

While management techniques have changed dramatically during this century, the lands of the Lewis and Clark National Forest remain gloriously unbridled. Adventure awaits those heading down any one of its hundreds of trails on foot, horseback, skis, or snowmobile. On the Rocky Mountain Division, hikers can make a vigorous six-mile climb to the fire lookout atop Steamboat Mountain, where the world falls away into the bold, rugged backcountry of the Scapegoat Wilderness. The South Fork Teton Trail, which climbs sharply to a point high above the Teton River, provides an equally demanding and dramatic climb. The less adventurous could make a trek to beautiful Mill Falls or hike along the Smith Creek Trail, stopping beside the string of

A pack string in the Bob Marshall Wilderness, above, winds its way through the lush meadows at the foot of the Chinese Wall. Most visitors to this part of the Bob Marshall come during the months of July and August. Those seeking solitude may want to head out either before the Fourth of July or after Labor Day.
CAL RYDER

A hunter searches for elk along the Rocky Mountain Front, left. This portion of the Lewis and Clark National Forest contains one of the finest bull elk populations in the state. KRISTI DUBOIS

crystal pools and waterfalls that line much of the route.

To the east, on the Jefferson Division, hikers can make an easy 1.6-mile amble to Memorial Falls or work their way up five miles of the Dry Wolf Trail to the spectacular Jefferson Divide. Other superb vistas can be seen by packing into the Smith River along Strawberry Ridge, climbing the easy path to Grandview Point high above shimmering Crystal Lake, or by heading to the high, wildflower-strewn meadows of the Windy Mountain Trail.

A float on the clear, cool Smith River provides one of the most engaging adventures on the Lewis and Clark National Forest. This popular river winds gently through the Big Belt and Little Belt mountains, much of it wrapped in wildflowers and lined by a stunning collage of limestone cliffs and palisades. The Montana Department of Fish, Wildlife and Parks monitors floating on the Smith, but a fair amount of the river flows unhurriedly through the lands of the Lewis and Clark National Forest.

When winter finally draws across the highlands of the Lewis and Clark, skiers and snowmobilers flock to the Little Belt Mountains. Just northeast of White Sulphur Springs, along U.S. Highway 89, is King's Hill Summit — one of several access points to the Neihart winter recreation area. More than 120 miles of

Rafters enjoy a quiet float through the canyons that line much of the clear Smith River, top left. The Smith flows through a portion of the Lewis and Clark National Forest. Floaters often spend several days — and nights — on a popular sixty-mile section of the river. MICHAEL S. SAMPLE

While about 12 million board feet of timber are sold each year on the Lewis and Clark National Forest, only a small amount still goes out by mule! Here a home builder skids out house logs from the forest west of Augusta, bottom left. KATIE BUMP

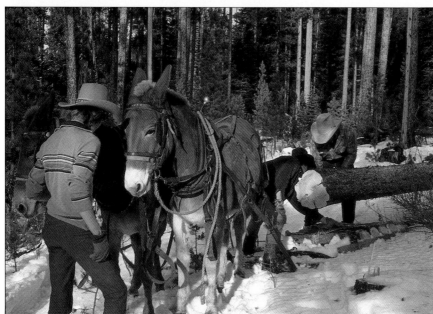

groomed and marked snowmobile trails cross this region. Many of the groomed routes, such as Upper King's Hill Ridge and Divide Road for snowmobiles and the Silver Crest Loops for skiers, offer traverses through quiet forest as well as wonderful views of the surrounding countryside. From these high perches, the world is a dazzling fantasy land — a white ocean of winter capped by a powder blue sky. Snow lays thick and soft on the conifers that line the trails, dropping off in the afternoon like icing left too long in the sun. People come from hundreds of miles to play each weekend at Neihart, one of the finest winter sports areas in all of Montana.

On the Rocky Mountain Division, winter sports enthusiasts head to the Rocky Mountain Hi ski and snowmobile area on the west fork of the Teton River, twenty-eight miles west of Choteau. Marias Pass, along U.S. Highway 2 just south of Glacier National Park, is another popular snowmobile and cross-country ski area in the division.

Winter here also forces much of the national forest's big game to seek the protection of lower elevations. The approximately 2,500 animals of the Sun River elk herd make their way from the Sun River Game Preserve (on land managed by the Lewis and Clark National Forest) through Sawmill Flats and along Willow Creek

A matched pair of long-tailed weasels plays on a log in the Lewis and Clark National Forest. Inquisitive, alert, and fearless, these creatures prey on smaller animals, birds, and insects. In the winter, their brown coats turn white, providing camouflage in the snow.
ALAN AND SANDY CAREY

MONTANA'S OWN GEMSTONE

Many who think of Montana as a place of legendary gold, silver, and copper strikes don't realize another equally spectacular treasure is tucked in the rolling limestone hills of the Little Belt Mountains. This range in the Lewis and Clark National Forest is the birthplace of the Yogo sapphire—a gemstone of such exquisite quality that it put central Montana on equal footing with the ruby mines of Burma and the emerald and diamond fields of Columbia and South Africa.

Yogo sapphires have made their way into major museums around the world and into the hands of everyone from Queen Victoria to President Harry Truman and from Kaiser Wilhelm to the British Royal Crown Jewel Collection. Although the much-touted sapphires of the Orient tend to be larger, they rarely match the Yogo's color and brilliance. In fact, many gemologists now consider the Yogo sapphire to set the world standard for excellence.

A century ago, no one went to the Little Belt Mountains looking for sapphires. The interest was so strong for gold and gold alone that most miners who found the little blue pebbles in their diggings simply threw them back into the creeks without further thought. But the casual efforts of a man named Jake Hoover first made the Yogo sapphire known to the outside world. Picking the stones up almost as an afterthought to gold-mining operations, Hoover and his partners eventually packed them in a cigar box and sent them to Tiffany & Company, where they caught the attention of America's foremost gem authority, Dr. Frederick Kunz. (Jake Hoover, incidentally, also stumbled across another national treasure of sorts. One day on his way home from a hunting trip, he came across a hungry, broke sixteen-year-old boy from St. Louis camped along the Judith River.

Hoover took the boy under his wing and, over the years, shared with him his love for the land and his vast knowledge of the frontier. That boy was the West's "Cowboy Artist," Charles M. Russell.)

In the end, the Yogo sapphire mines not only produced more wealth than all other American sapphire mines put together, but also outstripped the earnings of many a Rocky Mountain gold mine. The mining of sapphires along Yogo Creek continues to be good business today. (While visitors can pan for gold along many Lewis and Clark streams, Yogo sapphires occur only on patented mining claims or on private lands.)

Many experts feel the 7,000-foot-deep rock formation known as the "Yogo dike" still contains more gem-quality sapphires than any other deposit in the world. Indeed, despite its long and revered history, the best days of the Yogo sapphire may be yet to come.

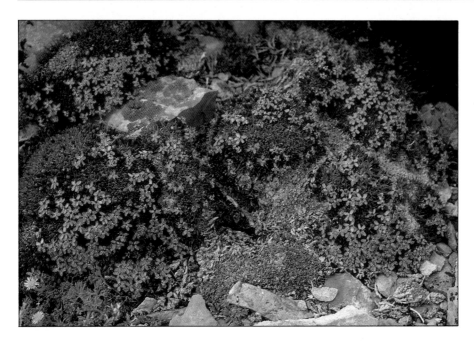

The blooms of moss campion will dazzle anyone who visits the alpine zones of the Rocky Mountain Front from early July to mid-August. This beautiful plant can be found in high tundra and mountainous regions around the world, from northern Canada to the Swiss Alps. KRISTI DUBOIS

to winter ranges at the Sun River Wildlife Management Area (on land managed by the state). The typically shallow snows here allow the elk to find food. Likewise, the Sun River bighorn sheep herd — one of the largest in the state, with eight hundred to one thousand animals — leaves the high country of the Bob Marshall Wilderness each fall for wintering grounds in the Sun River Canyon below Gibson Dam. Working with the Montana Department of Fish, Wildlife and Parks, the Lewis and Clark National Forest recently developed a special program to improve winter range grass growth for the Sun River bighorn herd by periodically burning certain portions of their winter range.

Those who visit the Lewis and Clark National Forest in May, June, and July will find much of the land blanketed with wildflowers. Different species unfold throughout the summer in slow, methodic stages, like the carefully orchestrated movements of a symphony. The wide range of climates here makes the Lewis and Clark symphony particularly varied and lovely. The show begins with pasque-flower, phlox, larkspur,

Bighorn rams butt heads in one of the most dramatic battles for social rank in all of nature. Each November, the crack of horns rings through the high country of the Lewis and Clark National Forest, which contains one of the largest bighorn sheep herds in the state. The ultimate winner of these contests is considered the dominant male. GLENN VAN NIMWEGEN

A high meadow in the Scapegoat Wilderness, below, erupts with wildflowers. In the background are the massive limestone ramparts of Scapegoat Mountain — an extension of the famed Chinese Wall located in the adjacent Bob Marshall Wilderness. DAVID MUENCH

spring beauties, and biscuitroot on the semi-arid slopes of the Jefferson Division, where a scant fourteen inches of moisture fall each year. Flowers blossom at higher and higher elevations as summer wears on, opening in the alpine zones of the Rocky Mountain Division sometime in July. Although the growing season lasts only six weeks in the extreme high country, these areas typically receive more than four times the moisture of lower elevations.

These high, snow-laden peaks make the Lewis and Clark a crucial watershed. Although the national forest contains barely three percent of the land area making

The grizzly bear, above, is one of many large mammals that make their home in the Lewis and Clark portion of the Scapegoat Wilderness. Those who travel in the Scapegoat should be familiar with proper backcountry procedures to protect themselves from unwanted encounters with this great animal. MICHAEL H. FRANCIS

From a distance, beargrass flowers, left, seem to float on their tall green stems like tufts of cream-colored cloud. Each beargrass plant blooms only once every several years. Without blossoms, the stalks resemble a vast field of very hearty grass. BILL CUNNINGHAM

up the Upper Missouri River watershed, it produces nearly one-fifth of that river's total annual surface flow. Throughout the early summer, water is slowly squeezed from the snowpack during the warmth of day and then held back as the chill of night descends. In this way, thousands of acres are irrigated — fed in more or less consistently measured amounts from the Sun, Smith, Judith, Musselshell, and Teton rivers.

This snowmelt, as well as the afternoon rain showers that fall on the forest through much of the summer, enable the Lewis and Clark to support domestic livestock grazing on almost 250,000 acres. In all, 15,000 cattle, 5,000 sheep, and 7,000 horses and mules graze these rich lands every year.

At the turn of the century, the "Lewis and Clark Forest Preserve" was a vast tract of land, taking in regions that today are part of the Kootenai and Flathead national forests and Glacier National Park. Although the Lewis and Clark has shrunk considerably, the 1.8 million acres it now contains remain wild and diverse. The variety in climate, elevation, wildlife, landforms, and vegetation provides the perfect setting for almost any outdoor activity. The Lewis and Clark National Forest remains an unforgettable segment of wild Montana and one of the shining jewels of the national forest system. ■

The land of the Rocky Mountain Front is a wilderness lover's dream — an unforgettable collage of cresting rock waves and timbered valleys that can steal the breath of even the most jaded mountain traveler. M. JAVORKA

LEWIS AND CLARK
NATIONAL FOREST DIRECTORY

POINTS OF INTEREST

SUN RIVER GAME PRESERVE is located within the Bob Marshall-Great Bear-Scapegoat Wilderness complex and provides an excellent place to see many big game animals, including elk, bighorn sheep, mountain goat, black and grizzly bears, moose, and white-tailed deer. Closed to hunting.

NEIHART WINTER SPORTS AREA is located northeast of White Sulphur Springs, in the Little Belt Mountains. Fine network of marked and groomed snowmobile and cross-country ski trails. Principal access at King's Hill Summit, along U.S. Highway 89.

MIDDLE FORK JUDITH RIVER is a 92,000-acre roadless area, ideal for fishing, hunting, and backpacking.

WILDERNESS AREAS

BOB MARSHALL 300,000 acres of the wilderness are located on this national forest. The extremely picturesque wilderness contains an excellent network of trails appropriate for use on horse, foot, or skis.

SCAPEGOAT 84,407 acres are located on the Lewis and Clark, adjacent to the Bob Marshall Wilderness. Both wilderness areas are defined by spectacular high mountains, lakes, and alpine wildflowers. Good climbing opportunities.

RECREATIONAL OPPORTUNITIES

HIKING AND RIDING More than sixty foot and horse trails scattered across the forest provide opportunities ranging from short day hikes to week-long outings. Trails are maintained from July 1 through November 15. Seven National Recreation Trails.

CAMPING Twenty-six campgrounds, generally open from late May to mid-September. Dispersed camping allowed on most forest lands.

RECREATIONAL CABINS Five cabins available during various times of the year. For more information, contact the Forest Supervisor's office.

RAFTING AND CANOEING Recommended floating season on the beautiful Smith River runs from mid-June to the end of July.

HUNTING Annual hunting seasons on the forest for mule deer, white-tailed deer, elk, black bear, grizzly bear, antelope, and mountain goat.

FISHING Good cutthroat trout waters in the Little Belt Mountains include Pilgrim, Deep, and Tenderfoot creeks and the headwaters of the Judith River. Badger and Birch creeks, South Fork of Two Medicine Creek, and the Sun, Dearborn, and Teton rivers are popular on the Rocky Mountain Division. Crystal, Forest, Wood, and Diversion lakes are all accessible by road. Fishing lakes reachable by trail include Hidden, Renshaw, Rhoda, and Bear lakes and Lake Levale.

ALPINE SKIING Showdown Ski Area (two chair lifts, one poma, and one rope tow), located thirty miles north of White Sulphur Springs. Rocky Mountain Hi Ski Area (one chair lift, one poma, and one rope tow), located twenty-eight miles west of Choteau at Teton Pass.

CROSS-COUNTRY SKIING Popular areas include the Silver Crest Trail System and the Neihart Recreation Area. Advanced skiers will enjoy the O'Brien Creek, Ranch Creek, and Deadman Ridge trails.

SNOWMOBILING Especially good opportunities at the Neihart Recreation Area. One groomed, 51-mile loop takes off here ("Loop A") and provides access to all other trails. Snow Play areas include O'Brien Park, Harley Park, Williams Park, and Moose Park, as well as areas along the Judith-Musselshell River Divide.

OFF-ROAD VEHICLES Good trail bike, mountain bike, and off-road vehicle opportunities in the Deep Creek-Tenderfoot Area, located north of Monarch. Both seasonal and vehicle-type restrictions may apply. Consult the Lewis and Clark National Forest visitors map for details.

ADMINISTRATIVE OFFICES

FOREST HEADQUARTERS 1101 Fifteenth St. N., Great Falls, MT 59403 (406) 791-7700

ROCKY MOUNTAIN RANGER DISTRICT Box 340, Choteau, MT 59422 (406) 466-5341

JUDITH RANGER DISTRICT Box 484, Stanford, MT 59479 (406) 566-2292

KINGS HILL RANGER DISTRICT Box A, White Sulphur Springs, MT 59645 (406) 547-3361

MUSSELSHELL RANGER DISTRICT Box F, Harlowton, MT 59036 (406) 632-4391

More than 175 years after Lewis and Clark first passed through the Gates of the Mountains on the Missouri River, the area remains a glorious destination for visitors to the Helena National Forest. The spot can be reached by trail, canoe, or on a tour boat that operates during summer months from the north shore of Upper Holter Lake. DAVID MUENCH

Helena

A land to explore

The enticing, often dramatic weave of mountains, meadow, and timber in the 976,000-acre Helena National Forest has long harbored countless species of wildlife and provided a setting for human activities of all types. People who comb these woods in search of deer and elk are adding new links to a chain of hunting that may have gone unbroken for eight thousand years. Recreational gold panners, still found each summer kneeling in eager anticipation beside rocky stream beds, hint at the gold fever that gripped the region more than 125 years ago. Numerous other activities have blossomed here, as well. A new generation of backpackers is setting off into the high, lonesome wilds that cradle 120 miles of the Continental Divide National Scenic Trail. Where Lewis and Clark once traveled up the Missouri River, water skiers and sail boarders can be found by the hundreds in July and August, skimming across the waters of Canyon Ferry Reservoir. Where men in buffalo robes once trekked across the high country in snowshoes, cross-country skiers now traverse the snowy shoulders of Stemple and MacDonald passes.

Given the long and varied use of these lands surrounding the beautiful and picturesque capital city of Helena, it's surprising so much of this national forest appears untracked and undiscovered. Those who wander slowly in July through the forested folds of the Elkhorn Mountains or hike along the stark limestone ridges that cap the Gates of the Mountains Wilderness will suddenly realize they've stumbled onto one of those wonderful slices of public land that has been all but overlooked by the modern traveler — a kind of solitary paradise, lost among Montana's sheer expanses of rock and grass and sky.

In large part because the Helena National Forest lies on either side of the Continental Divide in westcentral Montana, its lands boast especially diverse climates and landscapes. The western portion of the national forest actually straddles the Divide, running from the southern tip of the Bob Marshall Wilderness across dramatic 10,000-foot peaks to a point just east of Deer Lodge. Lovely blends of both meadow and timber are found here, with fine stands of Douglas-fir, western larch, and wind-shorn subalpine fir. The eastern portions of the national forest, on the other hand, drape across the lower, drier Big Belt Mountains, where the land is blanketed by sage, ponderosa pine, and lodgepole pine, with the lodgepole often rising from cool green coverings of grouse whortleberry.

The Helena's diversity allows for a variety of

Much of the Helena National Forest contains a splendid mix of rolling mountains covered with lodgepole pine, Douglas-fir, and grassy parklands. The lower, drier, eastern half of the forest is perfect for early season hiking and backpacking. BILL CUNNINGHAM

wildlife. Those interested in glimpsing some of the more magnificent big game should visit the 129,000-acre Elkhorn Wildlife Management Unit southeast of the city of Helena. These beautiful mountain lands, co-managed with the Montana Department of Fish, Wildlife and Parks, form the only Forest Service designated recreation and wildlife management area in the entire country. Grazing, timber harvesting, recreation, and mineral exploration all take place here. But managers also pay close attention to the animals — especially the thriving elk herd. Some of the wildlife

habitat improvements on the Elkhorn, such as the prescribed burning of sage fields to promote the growth of native grasses, has been paid for by the Rocky Mountain Elk Foundation. Visitors here also stand a good chance of catching frequent glimpses of mule and white-tailed deer, moose, black bear, and mountain goat. Mountain lions also call this region home, but both patience and luck are needed to actually spot these shy creatures.

Elsewhere on the Helena National Forest, those with binoculars are likely to spot both bighorn sheep and

EXPRESS ROUTE TO THE NORTH

Mention Rogers Pass to anyone who lives in central Montana, and they just might start shivering. This 5,470-foot crest along Montana Highway 200 has earned the dubious distinction of having the lowest recorded temperature in the 48 contiguous states — seventy degrees below zero, on January 20, 1954.

But more intriguing than its chilly temperatures is the role Rogers Pass plays as a raptor migration corridor. Perched on the lower east side of this pass from March 12 to April 3, 1988, researcher Fred Tilly watched a staggering 818 golden eagles and 129 bald eagles flashing

past on the heels of the west winds, most bound for nesting grounds in Canada. Tilly also counted fifty other raptors from his lookout, including red-tailed, sharp-shinned, and rough-legged hawks, as well as nearly 3,500 snow geese and more than five hundred tundra swans.

The consistent presence of 25- to 30-mile-per-hour winds along Rogers Pass offers, as Tilly put it, "an express route to the north." But this fast lane seems to be the preferred path only for strong fliers. Smaller birds, including immature golden eagles, sometimes lose their hold on these hearty winds and are

blown off course, out across the plains. In addition to steady winds, the Rogers Pass route also offers raptors good sources of food. Rabbits, ground squirrels, and other small rodents are plentiful along the entire eastern flank of the Front Range.

Rogers Pass may well become an important raptor tracking station, where researchers can gauge the general health of migratory golden eagle and bald eagle populations. Somehow it seems fitting that this pass, a silent icebox in the dead of winter, should each spring explode with such a flurry of life.

With wings spread wide, a bald eagle sails through a spring snow storm. Hundreds of bald and golden eagles migrate through Rogers Pass on Helena National Forest each spring.
TOM MANGELSEN

Hikers and horseback riders often travel through Refrigerator Canyon, located just off the Figure-8 route, as they head into the Gates of the Mountains Wilderness. Living up to its name, Refrigerator Canyon on some days may be twenty degrees cooler than the surrounding countryside. CRAIG AND LIZ LARCOM

mountain goats in the Gates of the Mountains Wilderness. Waterfowl and shore birds, as well as antelope, can be found along the perimeter of Canyon Ferry Reservoir. Many bald eagles spend the early part of winter in the Canyon Ferry area, between York Bridge and Canyon Ferry Dam, feeding on kokanee salmon. Wintering bald eagles can be seen along the Blackfoot River west of Lincoln, and golden eagles are frequently spotted at Avalanche Creek, as well as in the Big Belt Mountains at Hellgate Canyon.

Anglers will be interested to know that biologists recently discovered one of the largest pure strains of cutthroat trout in Montana on the Helena National Forest, in the cold, clear waters of the Little Blackfoot River. Sections of the Missouri River below Hauser Dam are revered by fishermen across the country for the trophy-sized brown trout — many of which weigh in at over fifteen pounds. Brook, rainbow, and bull trout are also plentiful here, as are arctic grayling and whitefish.

Visitors to the Helena can enjoy one of the national forest's finest recreational experiences along the Missouri River, just north of Upper Holter Lake. All summer, boat tours run through the magnificent canyon system known as the Gates of the Mountains — a towering limestone gorge whose walls are etched with the fossils of ocean life from more than 300 million years ago. This tapestry of rock, water, and sky was named by Meriwether Lewis on his expedition to the Pacific Ocean in the summer of 1805. Lewis was astonished at the canyon's overpowering atmosphere. "It is deep from side to side nor is there in the first three miles of this distance a spot except one of a few yards in extent on which a man could rest the soul of his foot.

Summer visitors to the mountains, especially to those places where the pine forests are broken by open meadows, sooner or later will be greeted by the mountain bluebird, above. These birds often build their nests in old woodpecker holes. MICHAEL H. FRANCIS

Horse travel is an increasingly popular way to see the backcountry of the Helena National Forest, left. In the Gates of the Mountains Wilderness alone, six trailheads are available for horse use, leading to more than fifty miles of trails. The Elkhorn Mountains and the area surrounding the Little Blackfoot River are also excellent places for horse trips. GEORGE WUERTHNER

From the singular appearance of this place I called it the gates of the Rocky Mountains."

Red-tailed hawks, eagles, osprey, and prairie falcons can be spotted at the the Gates of the Mountains, along with mergansers, grebes, bighorn sheep, river otters, and even an occasional loon. Those who journey through the Gates of the Mountains by concessionaire boat can make a leisurely stopover at the lovely Meriwether Picnic Area — the original campsite of the westward-bound Lewis and Clark party. Because this spot is accessible only by water or trail, it has retained a certain quiet, untrammeled beauty that few developed recreation sites enjoy. About a mile upstream from the picnic area is the idyllic Coulter Campground.

The Figure-8 route, about twenty miles east of the city of Helena, offers another stunning example of canyon scenery. This self-guided auto tour meanders past a magical collage of cliffs, canyons, mountains, old sapphire mines, and historical fire lookouts. A

The Figure- 8 Route — sprinkled with old saphhire mines, fire lookouts, limestone canyons, viewing points, and wildlife — is one of the most popular drives on the Helena National Forest.
GARRY WUNDERWALD

The diverse climates on the Helena National Forest give it a wide variety of tree and plant life, such as these aspen, left.
MICHAEL S. SAMPLE

Badgers, below, go after food underneath the ground with particular gusto. The animal's sharp claws and powerful front legs allow it to dig with surprising speed and efficiency.
ALAN D. CAREY

portion of the loop route has been closed indefinitely because of a washout along Trout Creek. But the water, wildlife, and scenery of places like Beaver Creek Canyon still make this route well worth the drive. Those wishing to pass through the washout area, which itself lies in the bottom of a lovely canyon, can do so either by foot or motorbike along a four-mile trail.

Hikers enjoy the Helena National Forest in part because it offers five access routes to the Continental Divide — good news for anyone wishing to sample some of the spectacular scenery along the Continental Divide National Scenic Trail. This hiking route, which when completed will stretch 3,100 magnificent miles from Canada to Mexico, winds its way through the high mountains of the Helena National Forest for 120 miles, passing within 13 miles of the city of Helena. Several of the Helena National Forest access points, including Stemple and MacDonald passes, have also become popular departure points for cross-country skiers.

While visitors may often feel they're venturing into untracked wild country, most of the Helena National Forest at one time or another has felt the eager feet of gold miners. The city of Helena itself grew up in an area known as "Last Chance Gulch," a name bestowed on the ravine where gold was discovered in 1864. The unusual nature of the Helena gold strike played a significant role in the area's permanent settlement. Rather than only placer metals, miners found large deposits of granite-bound gold and silver embedded in veins of quartz. Extracting such riches called for larger, long-term mining operations — the kind that quickly gave Helena the kind of stable population few other gold towns could muster.

More than one hundred years and millions of dollars in gold later, mining continues to play an important role

Mule deer, or "mulies" as they're sometimes called, earned their name because of their large, black-fringed ears, top right. The many clearings on the Helena National Forest that support healthy shrub growth make perfect habitats for these graceful animals. HARRY ENGELS

Each year hundreds of people head to the Helena National Forest to cut Christmas trees, bottom right. CRAIG AND LIZ LARCOM

on the Helena National Forest. As was true so long ago, the majority of today's mining efforts seek gold and silver, which many experts believe still exist on these national forest lands in sizable quantities.

Oil and gas exploration also occurs on the Helena National Forest. Much of the national forest sits over the western Overthrust Belt — a geological formation that in places holds great petroleum reserves and has

The Helena National Forest is a place of both bold grandeur and delicate beauty. Often the tiniest nooks and crannies, such as this small portion of Wolf Creek in the Big Belt Mountains, in the end prove to be the most unforgettable. DAVID MUENCH

created interest in oil and gas exploration and leasing on the Helena National Forest.

National forest officials now face the challenge of balancing mining and oil and gas development with an increasing demand for recreation. Visitors from nearby Missoula, Bozeman, and Great Falls, as well as from other states, are starting to realize the Helena holds rich recreational opportunities for hunting, hiking, skiing, snowmobiling, fishing, and off-highway vehicle use. This national forest's attributes likely will make it a favorite spot in years to come for those who love the Rocky Mountain out-of-doors. ∎

One of the surest and most beautiful signs of spring on the Helena National Forest is the appearance of fairyslippers, top right. Also known as calypso orchids, these lovely flowers appear soon after the snow melts. With sufficient moisture, they will last well into summer.
PETE AND ALICE BENGEYFIELD

Visitors who spend much time around slow-moving streams, rivers, and lower elevation lake shores are likely to meet up with the painted turtle, bottom right.
DAVE McGEE

HELENA
NATIONAL FOREST DIRECTORY

POINTS OF INTEREST

GATES OF THE MOUNTAINS is a splendid canyon cut by the Missouri River through more than one thousand feet of rock. Good bird life. Accessible by trail from Gates of the Mountains Wilderness or by concessionaire boat. The tour boat departure site is well marked from Interstate 15, approximately sixteen miles north of Helena.

MT. BALDY AREA contains sixteen thousand unroaded acres, surrounding the 9,472-foot Mt. Baldy. Located northeast of Townsend. High mountain lakes and hiking trails.

WILDERNESS AREAS

GATES OF THE MOUNTAINS 28,562 acres rich in limestone cliffs and deep, rugged canyons. Despite its location barely twenty miles from downtown Helena, it remains the least used wilderness in Montana.

SCAPEGOAT 80,697 acres on the Helena, characterized by broad expanses of alpine and subalpine country and the spectacular mountains of the Continental Divide. Access by trails only. Contains trails for hikers and horseback riders.

RECREATIONAL OPPORTUNITIES

HIKING AND RIDING 733 miles of trails, including excellent access to the Continental Divide and a portion of the Continental Divide National Scenic Trail. Popular horse routes include Snowbank-Liverpool Trail 418, Stonewall Ridge Trail 417, and Porcupine Basin Trail 488.

CAMPING Eleven developed campgrounds. Dispersed camping allowed in much of the forest.

RECREATIONAL CABINS Kading Cabin, south of Elliston, available from approximately December 15 through the end of March. For more information, contact the Helena Ranger District.

SCENIC DRIVES The Figure-8 route, an 85-mile auto tour, winds through the Big Belt Mountains northeast of Helena. A four-mile portion of the drive through Trout Canyon has been washed out, so driving the entire loop is no longer possible.

HUNTING Fine elk and deer populations. Also pronghorn, black bear, mountain goat, bighorn sheep, and moose.

FISHING Several species of trout found on the forest, as well as whitefish, arctic grayling, and Dolly Varden. Fine cutthroat trout fishing in the Little Blackfoot River, as well as at Park Lake. Kokanee salmon and trophy brown trout in the Missouri River below Hauser Dam.

CROSS-COUNTRY SKIING Good, but ungroomed, trails at Stemple Pass on the Lincoln Ranger District and MacDonald Pass on the Helena Ranger District.

SNOWMOBILING Approximately 220 miles of trails, including popular routes near Lincoln on the Lincoln Ranger District, at the Marysville-Austin and Rimini-Elliston-Basin trail systems on the Helena Ranger District, and at the Magpie Area east of Canyon Ferry Lake on the Townsend Ranger District.

OFF-ROAD VEHICLES All trails open to mountain and trail bikes except those within wilderness areas. Contact individual ranger districts for more information.

ADMINISTRATIVE OFFICES

FOREST HEADQUARTERS 301 S. Park, Drawer 10014, Federal Office Building, Helena, MT 59626 (406) 449-5201

TOWNSEND RANGER DISTRICT 415 S. Front, Box 29, Townsend, MT 59644 (406) 266-3425

LINCOLN RANGER DISTRICT Highway 200, Box 234, Lincoln, MT 59639 (406) 362-4265

HELENA RANGER DISTRICT 2001 Poplar, Helena, MT 59601 (406) 449-5490

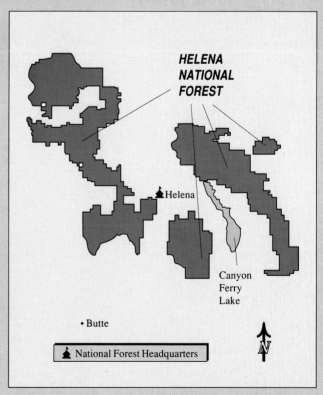

HELENA NATIONAL FOREST

Helena

Canyon Ferry Lake

• Butte

▲ National Forest Headquarters

N

Among the diverse habitats of the Deerlodge National Forest, none is more productive than its riparian zones. Lakeshores and stream banks are popular not only with recreationists, but with a wide variety of birds, fish, and mammals. MICHAEL S. SAMPLE

Deerlodge

Where there's room for work and play

Perhaps no federal land reserve in the country could put a bigger smile on the face of Gifford Pinchot than the Deerlodge National Forest. Pinchot, America's first trained forester and the first chief of the Forest Service, championed the notion of "multiple use" on federal forest reserves. That idea called for managing the resources of public forest lands — the timber, grass, water, and minerals — in a way that would offer the greatest sustained economic good to the largest number of people.

Almost from the time that James and Granville Stuart set up the first sluice boxes in Montana on Gold Creek in 1852, the region that would one day include the Deerlodge National Forest has been a busy, hard-working kind of place. The region's economy and recreation have been fixed to these federal lands for a period well beyond the memories of most people living today in Butte, Philipsburg, Anaconda, or the twenty other towns adjacent to or within the boundaries of the Deerlodge National Forest. Mining for gold, silver, and copper has always been popular on this national forest in southwest Montana. And throughout the first thirty years of the twentieth century, timber from the Deerlodge provided shoring for mine shafts and, later, fuel for heating homes and running copper smelters. At one point, nearly five hundred men roamed the forested hills outside of Butte, felling timber for the booming city down below. A great many of the early ranchers who supplied beef to all those miners grazed their cattle on national forest lands, as ranchers continue to do today. And farmers have long used water from the Deerlodge National Forest to irrigate their crops.

The relationship local communities have had with this 1.2 million-acre national forest continues today, although a significant amount of the interaction now comes in the form of recreation. And that's easy to understand. Straddling the Continental Divide and embracing eight separate mountain ranges, the Deerlodge quite literally has something for everyone: more than 1,000 miles of fishing streams, 140 lakes, 22 campgrounds, 629 miles of foot, horse, and motorcycle trails, 234 miles of marked snowmobile trails, 40 miles of marked ski trails, 43,629 acres of wilderness, the Discovery Basin downhill ski area, and landscapes that vary from low, rolling, semi-arid grasslands to rugged, rocky peaks towering far above timberline. The proximity of Butte, as well as the easy access provided to residents of Bozeman, Missoula, and Helena by Interstates 90 and 15, help make the Deerlodge one of the more popular national forests in the Northern Region. In fact, the Deerlodge consistently logs more than one million recreation visitor days each year. Georgetown Lake alone, a lovely forest recreation complex located along the Pintler Scenic Route (Montana Highway 1), records a full four percent of all lake fishing in Montana.

The Deerlodge contains recreational opportunities of all kinds, from campgrounds and picnic grounds to hiking, cross-country ski, and snowmobile trails. But it can take particular pride in the Sheepshead Mountain Recreation Area, located just nine miles north of Butte. Over the years, this area has become known as one of the finest handicapped-accessible recreation areas in the country. Developed as a cost-share program with the help of eighteen separate organizations, Sheepshead Mountain today offers superb camping and picnicking opportunities, as well as 4.5 miles of paved trails designed for use by people in wheelchairs. In 1988 alone, more than ten thousand people used the Sheepshead Mountain facilities.

The long, steady use of the Deerlodge National Forest has made careful management of the resources necessary. With its rich deposits of gold, silver, tungsten, copper, and antimony, the Deerlodge has been the leader of Montana "hard rock" mining for more than eighty years. And with a new wave of more efficient extraction technologies, exploration isn't likely to slow down soon. In 1988, forest managers approved sixty-two new plans of operation for projects of all sizes. Near Fleecer Mountain on the Butte Ranger District, the Pegasus Gold Corporation is spending $25 million to develop a 400-acre mine expected to process 5,000 tons of ore a day and yield 35,000 ounces of gold each year. The Deerlodge National Forest worked

A wary lynx, left, patrols its territory. Sporting large, padded feet, lynx can move with surprising swiftness and grace even in deep snow. ALAN AND SANDY CAREY

A close-up look at crested beardtongue, below, reveals fine filaments, or hairs, within the showy blossom. This tall flower grows from the foothills to timberline. MICHAEL S. SAMPLE

closely with Pegasus to lessen the visual impacts of such a large operation, as well as the effects on area wildlife, soils, and water.

While charged with regulating this and other mining activity, the Deerlodge also is repairing damage done during the more footloose mining era of a half-century ago. Heavy gold-dredging activities actually lowered the water tables beneath several rich meadow areas on the national forest, ultimately causing their surfaces to dry out and the natural enclosure banks to cave in around them. Land managers are repairing this damage by installing small check dams to slow sedimentation and raise the water levels. And efforts are underway to plant willows to help stabilize eroded stream banks.

Deerlodge managers also must monitor logging on the national forest, which sells close to 25 million board feet of timber each year — among the highest cuts of any national forest in the immediate area. Forest biologists use new wildlife research models to structure timber sales in a way that will have minimal effects on the region's magnificent elk herds, which are watched closely by thousands of sportsmen. The Fleecer Mountain area west of Butte has the second-highest concentration of hunters per acre of any area in Montana.

The Deerlodge's diverse habitat — a splendid mix of high alpine zones, bunchgrass range, old-growth forest, streamside willow corridors, and wetlands — contains more than 150 native species of mammals, fish, birds, and reptiles. Its big game herds include antelope, moose, mule deer, mountain goat, black bear, and bighorn sheep. According to U.S. Fish and

Sun lights up the rugged flanks of 10,464-foot Mount Warren, in the Anaconda-Pintler Wilderness. LARRY ULRICH

A ROCKY MOUNTAIN HIGH

Although only one-third of the rugged Anaconda-Pintler Wilderness is actually managed by the Deerlodge National Forest, more than half the people who enter this magnificent area use one of the six Deerlodge entryways. This high mountain preserve takes the first half of its name from the Anaconda Mountains and the second from trapper Charles Pintler, who set up house in the Big Hole Valley in 1885.

Even within the state of Montana, the Anaconda-Pintler Wilderness has none of the name recognition of its distant neighbors — the Bob Marshall to the north, the Absaroka-Beartooth to the southeast, the Selway-Bitterroot to the west. The lack of recognition is rather remarkable, considering the incredible mix of forests, sparkling lakes, and high alpine meadows found here. From low, sage-covered foothills, the land rises more than five thousand feet to the crown of the Continental Divide.

Hikers standing on the summits of the Pintler Peaks or Rainbow Mountain are surrounded by the essence of true Rocky Mountain high country. From here, they can view the U-shaped valleys that dominate the landscape, carved out thousands of years ago by steely blue tongues of glacial ice. The clearest of mountain streams run through many of the valleys. Permanent snowfields lie stark against sheer slopes of jumbled gray talus. In August, the high meadows glow with wildflowers, as dozens of plants race to bloom within the confines of a summer barely eight weeks long.

The Anaconda-Pintler contains 280 miles of Forest Service trails, including forty-five spectacular miles that shadow the 10,000-foot crest of the Continental Divide. While most of the footpaths are in good shape, hikers should be aware that lodgepole and whitebark pine trees killed by a pine beetle infestation in the early 1930s are now falling in some places, making travel more strenuous than usual. Maps of the Anaconda-Pintler Wilderness can be purchased in any office of the Deerlodge, Bitterroot, or Beaverhead national forests, which share management of the area.

The 158,516-acre Anaconda-Pintler Wilderness is sometimes called Montana's "forgotten wilderness," because it receives such light use. But those who visit it don't forget it.
MICHAEL S. SAMPLE

Porcupines are adept climbers and are one of the most common residents of Montana's national forests. Their backs are covered with sharp quills, providing protection from would-be predators even when they are ambling on the ground. JEFFREY T. HOGAN

An elk calf sports a thick coat of winter frost. In the winter, elk migrate to lower elevations where lighter snowfall allows them better access to food. TOM MURPHY

Wildlife Service criteria, the Deerlodge has no habitat for threatened or endangered species. But sightings of grizzly bears and wolves have been confirmed.

Like the elk herds, the bighorn sheep of the Deerlodge have attracted national, and even international, attention. Each year, the state of Montana auctions off one permit to hunt a Rocky Mountain bighorn sheep from one of the state's best herds. That prize has been known to go for as much as $100,000, with the state using the money for habitat improvement, research, and management activities involving bighorn sheep. The permit often has been filled with a sheep from one of the three herds living on the Deerlodge National Forest, where rams grow especially large and heavy horns.

Thousands of anglers also come to the Deerlodge, which has more than one thousand miles of fishable streams. The national forest contains portions of the upper stretches of Rock Creek, long known for its world-class fishing.

Hikers on the Deerlodge have plenty of opportunity to view splendid scenery. Significant portions of the Tobacco Root, Flint Creek, Highland, Sapphire, Elkhorn, and Anaconda ranges lie on this forest. All are worth several days of slow, deliberate exploration. The 45-mile Highline Trail passes through much of the pristine Deerlodge portion of the Anaconda-Pintler Wilderness. And a 150-mile section of the Continental Divide National Scenic Trail also passes through here.

Visitors also can make use of two fine cabins available through the recreational cabin rental program. Doney Lake Cabin is located eleven miles northwest of the town of Deer Lodge and managed by the Deerlodge Ranger District, while the Hells Canyon Cabin is thirty miles southwest of Whitehall and managed by the Jefferson Ranger District.

With its rich resources, the Deerlodge no doubt will continue to be a hard-working, hard-playing forest in the years to come — carrying on its long and varied tradition of use. ■

The rolling, open parklands on much of the Deerlodge National Forest provide perfect spots for a fast trip on a clipper sled, saucer, or inner tube. Several winter sports — including snowmobiling and skiing — are popular on the national forest, especially around Georgetown Lake. ALAN AND SANDY CAREY

NEW LEVELS OF COMPROMISE

Managing America's national forests has never been an easy proposition. But where early struggles centered around a basic lack of money and manpower to fight fires and enforce regulations, problems today are much more complex. Managers deciding how best to use the national forests' resources must balance the concerns of various interest groups, many of which make conflicting demands.

Such conflicts were present when the Deerlodge National Forest came up with its forest plan. Dissatisfaction with the plan led to six federal appeals from the timber industry, which felt too little timber would be harvested under the proposal. Meanwhile, conservationists filed nine appeals, based on their concerns that timber harvesting and road building could encroach on existing roadless areas.

Then in the spring of 1989, a rather remarkable event occurred. In an unprecedented series of meetings, forest officials, conservation leaders, and timber industry representatives hammered out an agreement outlining the use and protection of the Deerlodge in the years ahead. As a result, all fifteen appeals were withdrawn.

Conservationists agreed not to oppose timber sales totaling fifteen million board feet, which they had felt violated roadless areas. The timber industry must abide by new procedures for wildlife and water quality protection. Both the timber industry and conservation groups pressed for the construction of temporary logging roads that can be reclaimed after the trees are harvested, rather than the permanent roads the Forest Service has required in the past. This change will save the timber industry money, while addressing conservationist concerns that lands may not be eligible for wilderness designation simply because they have existing roads.

Of course, the real test of how smoothly these new guidlelines will work is yet to come. But it's hard not to feel somewhat optimistic when any national forest ends up in compromise instead of combat. The Deerlodge plan provides a clear glimmer of hope for the future.

DEERLODGE
NATIONAL FOREST DIRECTORY

POINTS OF INTEREST

GEORGETOWN LAKE is set between the Flint Creek Range to the north and the Pintler Mountains to the south. The Deerlodge's busiest recreation site, it contains campgrounds, picnic areas, boat ramps, a marina, and trailheads offering quick access to the surrounding backcountry. Excellent fishing.

SHEEPSHEAD MOUNTAIN RECREATION AREA is a 140-acre site designed for disabled people. It includes a playground, wading pond, fishing pier, paved trails, and a handicapped-accessible campground. Natural highlights include a small lake, three streams, and a fine braid of meadow lands.

WILDERNESS AREAS

ANACONDA-PINTLER 44,175 acres located on the Deerlodge National Forest. The wilderness straddles the Continental Divide, with elevations varying by more than five thousand feet. High lakes, cirque valleys, and steep, sheer canyons.

RECREATIONAL OPPORTUNITIES

HIKING AND RIDING About six hundred miles of trails, with particularly good hiking and riding opportunities in the Anaconda-Pintler Wilderness and the Tobacco Root and Elkhorn mountains. The Continental Divide National Scenic Trail will pass through the national forest.

CAMPING Twenty-two campgrounds, some of which are open into October. Dispersed camping is allowed on most of the forest.

RECREATIONAL CABINS Doney Lake Cabin, eleven miles northwest of Deer Lodge, and Hells Canyon Cabin, thirty miles southwest of Whitehall, can be rented all year.

SCENIC DRIVES Montana Highway 38, a gravel road, crosses Skalkaho Pass west of Georgetown Lake and enters the Bitterroot National Forest. It drops along Daly Creek and past Skalkaho Falls toward Hamilton. Two campgrounds on the east side of the pass.

HUNTING Blue grouse, moose, black bear, mule deer, and elk.

FISHING Cutthroat, rainbow, and brook trout populations in many of the high country lakes and streams. Georgetown Lake also contains kokanee salmon and bull trout.

ALPINE SKIING Discovery Basin (two chair lifts and two pony lifts), located north of Georgetown Lake.

CROSS-COUNTRY SKIING Forty miles of marked cross-country ski trails. Nice trails in the Whitetail-Haystack Roadless Area northeast of Butte.

SNOWMOBILING More than 230 miles of signed trails. Popular areas include the East Fork Reservoir/Georgetown Lake Area on the Philipsburg Ranger District (39 miles of groomed trails), the Continental Divide/Leadville Area on the Jefferson and Deer Lodge ranger districts (40 miles of groomed trails), and the Lowlands Area on the Butte Ranger District (46 miles of groomed trails).

OFF-ROAD VEHICLES All roads and trails open to off-road vehicles unless posted otherwise.

ADMINISTRATIVE OFFICES

FOREST HEADQUARTERS Federal Building, Box 400, Butte, MT 59703 (406) 496-3400

PHILIPSBURG RANGER DISTRICT P.O. Box H, Philipsburg, MT 59858 (406) 859-3211

JEFFERSON RANGER DISTRICT 405 W. Legion, P.O. Box F, Whitehall, MT 59759 (406) 287-3223

BUTTE RANGER DISTRICT 2201 White Blvd., Butte, MT 59701 (406) 494-2147

DEER LODGE RANGER DISTRICT 91 Frontage Road, Deer Lodge, MT 59722 (406) 846-1770

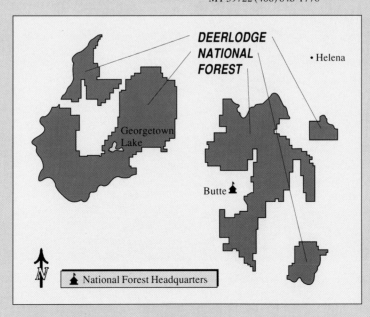

The 10,220-foot Antone Peak reaches for the Montana sky from the aptly named Snowcrest Range, which stretches about twenty miles from north to south. TIM EGAN

Beaverhead

*Tinged
with a
frontier
flavor*

The Beaverhead National Forest may top the list of anyone pressed to name one national forest in Montana that captures the far-ranging splendor of the northern Rockies, one where the land shines with just a little more of that wild, dizzy innocence that marked the days of the American frontier. The tributaries of most of the major Missouri River feeder streams — the Jefferson, the Madison, the Big Hole, and the Beaverhead — still drift through mile after mile of unpopulated countryside. Moose still wander undisturbed through the willows that lie thick along the Ruby River, while the mountain goats of Big Sheep Creek Basin rarely spy any people from their perches. Many of the trails that were here one hundred years ago have been widened into gravel roads, but crossing much of this southwest Montana national forest by automobile remains a wonderfully slow and deliberate affair. It's still possible here to feel marvelously overwhelmed by the remote features of the surrounding land.

The fact is, far more human hustle and bustle occurred in this area one hundred years ago than does today. Much is made of the fact the Bozeman Trail was a main thoroughfare for emigrants bound for the gold fields of Bannack and Virginia City. Yet dangers posed by angry Indians all but shut down the route after only three years. The vast majority of would-be miners who poured into the region did so along a road running north from Fort Hall on the Oregon Trail, passing through or adjacent to lands that now make up the Beaverhead National Forest. A great portion of the Beaverhead's more than 2.1 million acres acted both as an entryway and a final destination for thousands of adventurers who fashioned the glory years of old Montana.

This route from the Oregon Trail to the wide, grassy valleys of the Beaverhead country also helped give birth to the Montana cattle industry. In 1858, a man named Richard Grant had the bright notion of trading for haggard, trail-weary cattle on the Oregon Trail, driving them north to winter on the rich carpets of grass along the Beaverhead River, and then bringing them south again in the spring to sell at a substantial profit.

Later, the discovery of gold in the region created an even better market for good beef. As many a savvy rancher discovered, cattle and horses often were far surer pathways to riches than was gold.

Today, ranching continues to be important on the Beaverhead. More than 900,000 sheep, cattle, and horses graze on these national forest lands each year.

The Beaverhead is known for its ability to produce grass. But managing the range for use by such large numbers of domestic animals is not necessarily an easy task. As more development occurs on privately held elk wintering range, for example, national forest managers must manage more areas primarily for winter wildlife forage. Livestock also tend to trample

Cattle have always been big business on the lands of the Beaverhead National Forest, above, partly because hay can be grown easily on the valley bottoms. This hay is so high in protein that it was once shipped all the way to Kentucky and Tennessee as feed for race horses. TIM EGAN

The bold profile of 10,876-foot Sphinx Mountain, left, rises from the high, windswept crest of the Madison Range. At its feet lie beautiful parklands and thick blankets of lodgepole pine — home to elk, bighorn sheep, and grizzly bears. GEORGE WUERTHNER

down vegetation along streams and rivers, sometimes causing the soils to wash into the waters. More than two dozen ongoing projects on the Beaverhead are designed to help restore damaged watersheds. Some of these, such as the livestock exclosure fence around Rabbia Creek, were accomplished with the help of Forest Service volunteers.

Despite providing range for so much livestock, the Beaverhead has plenty of room for recreationists, too. Visitors can find themselves far from the madding crowds with little effort. The sixty-mile gravel road system known as the Gravelly Range Scenic Loop, for instance, overflows with long, lonely vistas and thick carpets of high mountain wildflowers in July. This drive allows visitors to feast their eyes on a wide reach of Montana high country, from the Centennial Mountains to the Anacondas, and also offers glimpses into much of the wild country surrounding Yellowstone and Grand Teton national parks. Forest Road 484, a National Scenic Byway connecting the towns of Wise River and Polaris, wanders through the lush, high reaches of the Pioneer Mountains. This drive provides excellent opportunities for spotting moose during winter months. Travelers also can take advantage of five campgrounds along the route, as well as a commercial hot springs resort and enough trailheads to keep walkers busy for weeks.

The Crystal Park Picnic Area makes a particularly interesting stop along the Wise River-to-Polaris route. True to the name, large crystals of garnet and various other minerals abound here, formed by molten granite pushing its way into beds of limestone nearly 70 million years ago. Devoted rockhounds of all ages stop here, and the national forest allows small-scale digging

The rich riparian habitats on the Beaverhead National Forest provide fertile ground for the growth of willows, a key soil stabilizer and an important food for both beaver and moose. MICHAEL S. SAMPLE

for these crystals at no charge.

Some of the same brew of ancient geology that produced the beautiful rocks of Crystal Park also created veins of silver in many parts of the Pioneer Mountains. The old Elkhorn Mine lies less than three air miles east of Crystal Park and is reachable in high-clearance vehicles via an old mining road. Ore was first extracted from the Elkhorn Mine in the 1870s. Final processing into metal actually occurred in Wales, with the ore first taken by bull team to Utah, then by rail to San Francisco, and finally by ship to the British Isles. In the early part of the twentieth century, after a rollercoaster ride of rising and falling silver prices, the Elkhorn Mine was taken over by William Allen. Allen not only constructed one of Montana's first million dollar mills, but also the town of Coolidge (named after friend President Calvin Coolidge). From 1922 to 1932,

the village bustled with stores, homes, a school, post office, cookhouse, surveyor's office, railroad depot, and pool hall. Today Coolidge is a lovely, sagging old ghost town, set high in the pines beneath the rugged spires of Saddleback Mountain. The crumbling homes, stables, and various mine buildings sing a lonely, haunting song — a familiar refrain about the grand dreams that have come and gone in the shadows of these magnificent mountains. Skiers and snowmobilers should note that Coolidge has a special appeal in winter, when the hush of deep snow softens the rough edges of the old town.

Visitors who find themselves hooked by the beauty of the Pioneer Mountain trails may also want to consider making forays into the Tendoy, Beaverhead, and Gravelly ranges, as well as into the portions of two wilderness areas that lie on the Beaverhead National

At Crystal Park, located twenty-nine miles south of Wise River on the Wise River-to-Polaris Road, visitors can dig for both amethyst and smokey quartz crystals. A picnic area is located adjacent to the digging grounds.
MICHAEL S. SAMPLE (both)

FOR RENT: SPARTAN ROOMS, WITH ATMOSPHERE

The more than three dozen rustic cabins and lookout towers available for rent on Montana's national forests provide one of the greatest, yet least known, opportunities for recreationists. For fees ranging from fifteen to twenty dollars per day, visitors who have spent their days hiking, skiing, or snowmobiling can spend their nights wrapped in the warm, wooded solitude of a historic backcountry field station or perched high in the clouds in an old fire tower.

Most of these units are best described as primitive, offering little more than a table, chairs, bunks, and, in most cases, cooking utensils and firewood. Water usually must be treated or boiled before drinking, and outhouses are the order of the day. But the accommodations are sufficient for those seeking the chance to straddle some glorious high cleft of the Rockies or immerse themselves for a week in the thick of a backcountry forest.

The Beaverhead National Forest currently has twelve cabins available for rent — second in number only to the Gallatin National Forest. The Canyon Creek Cabin, located thirteen miles west of Melrose, can be rented year-round, while other units are open anywhere from three to eleven months of the year. For instance, Bloody Dick, a remote cabin located in the shadow of the Continental Divide, is open weekends only from December 1 through March 31.

The ease with which the cabins can be reached varies widely. Birch Creek Cabin, open from December 5 through March 31, is a scant one-fourth mile from a plowed road. Horse Prairie Guard Station, set in sweeping high plateau country and available for approximately the same period, can be reached in just 1.5 miles. On the other hand, depending on snow conditions, reaching Bloody Dick Cabin may require a 23-mile trek by snowmobile or ski.

The cabin rental program provides a wonderful opportunity for the public, as well as a chance for the Forest Service to preserve these historical structures for years to come. Money collected from rental fees remains within the rental program and is used for the upkeep or restoration of the units. Permits are required for the use of all cabins and lookouts and can be obtained by mail or in person through the individual ranger districts that administer the sites. A complete list of the available lookouts and cabins in the Northern Region can be obtained by writing the Regional Office of the Forest Service at: Federal Building, P.O. Box 7669, Missoula, MT 59807.

Cabins are inventoried and checked for cleanliness by each new visitor. Those who fail to leave them in good order are not allowed to rent again. But the vast majority of people who use these cabins and lookouts see them as a kind of special gift. They not only pack out or burn every bit of trash, but leave a good supply of kindling for the next person who walks cold and tired through the door. Some visitors leave a little extra dry or canned food for that time when someone runs short. If handled with care, the cabin and lookout rental program will continue to be one of the most precious recreational assets of Montana's national forests.

The 35-mile trek from Grasshopper Valley to Wise River in the Pioneer Mountains makes for a fine snowmobile trip. Other popular snowmobiling areas include a route from Virginia City to Clover Meadows in the Gravelly Range and along the southeast side of the Tobacco Root Mountains.
M. RYAN

White in the winter and brown in the summer, a snowshoe hare, above left, adapts to changing conditions. Although cottontail rabbits may be found in some Montana national forests, the snowshoe hare — named for its long, fur-covered feet — is far more common on the Beaverhead National Forest and most others.
MICHAEL H. FRANCIS

The bright flowers of Indian paintbrush decorate a mountain meadow on the Beaverhead National Forest, above right. This flower may be found virtually all summer, lingering even into late August at high elevations. MICHAEL S. SAMPLE

Wise River pours out of the Pioneer Mountains in the Beaverhead National Forest, left. For most of its length, Wise River is paralleled by the Wise River-Polaris Scenic Byway, part of the new National Forest Scenic Byway system.
MICHAEL S. SAMPLE

Forest. A trek into the Anaconda-Pintler Wilderness, climbing from Pintler Campground to the mosaic of meadow and mountain surrounding Pintler Pass, provides a memorable experience. The Beaverhead also contains a portion of the 250,000-acre Lee Metcalf Wilderness, an extremely rugged and pristine area with a striking collection of sheer peaks planted in thick forests of Douglas-fir, lodgepole pine, and Engelmann spruce. Both wilderness areas have the feel of classic alpine country — a world away from the central portions of the national forest, where much of the land is composed of soft-shouldered, 10,000-foot swells of grass and sage.

The threads of history that run through this forest are as significant as any in Montana. In August 1805, the Lewis and Clark expedition was trudging southwestward along the willow-laden banks of the Beaverhead River, in desperate need of horses. "Without horses," wrote Lewis, "we shall be obliged to leave a great part of our stores, of which, it appears to me that we have a stock already sufficiently small for the length of the voyage before us." Then on August 8, not far from present-day Dillon, the Shoshone woman named Sacajawea spotted a rock formation she

Among the waterfowl that frequent the Beaverhead National Forest lands is the spectacular trumpeter swan — the largest of all American waterfowl. Brought back from the edge of extinction in 1932, the trumpeter population now includes five hundred birds that nest in the greater Yellowstone ecosystem. JESS R. LEE

Moose frequent many of the stream bottoms in the Beaverhead National Forest, top right. While they may look gangly and uncoordinated, these remarkable creatures can run at speeds of up to thirty-five miles an hour and swim much faster than any human. GLENN VAN NIMWEGEN

Snow in the fall forces mule deer, bottom right, down out of the high country. Visitors stand the best chance of seeing large bucks like this one in the hour immediately after dawn, just after sunset, and on moonlit nights.
ALAN AND SANDY CAREY

recognized as "the beaver's head" (now a state monument along Montana Highway 41). The explorers had arrived, she announced confidently, in the land of her people, the Shoshone. Fresh horses were close at hand.

Also located nearby was Lemhi Pass, a small saddle on the crest of the Continental Divide. It was on this pass, located on what is now the Idaho border at the extreme fringes of the Beaverhead National Forest, that the expedition finally gazed on waters that ran not east but west, bound for the Pacific Ocean. Following a tiny rivulet of water up to the great Divide, one of the expedition members stood with a foot on each side and, according to Lewis, "thanked his god that he had lived to bestride the mighty and heretofor deemed endless Missouri."

Today visitors can hike, bicycle, or drive a dirt roadway that climbs through the national forest up to Lemhi Pass. Thousands of acres of wildflowers, including balsam root, wyethia, lupine, cinquefoil, and paintbrush, surround the summit area. The view from the top of Lemhi Pass is exquisite — range after range of high, forested mountains, rising and falling against the far horizon like the crests of ocean waves. It's easy here to feel that level of vast, untarnished wildness that has become a kind of trademark for the Beaverhead National Forest — a bold portrait of mountains and sky that will stir all who pass this way. ■

For more than forty years, Smokey the Bear has been a
national symbol for the prevention of forest fires. Here, he
makes a special appearance at a Halloween parade in the
town of Wisdom, top. BEAVERHEAD NATIONAL FOREST PHOTO

Cross-country skiers carve a trail on a snowy hillside in
the Beaverhead National Forest. In many national forests,
including the Beaverhead, skiers and snowmobilers can
enjoy a comfortable backcountry cabin at the end of their
journey, thanks to the Forest Service's cabin-rental
program. MICHAEL S. SAMPLE

BEAVERHEAD
NATIONAL FOREST DIRECTORY

POINTS OF INTEREST

EAST AND WEST PIONEER ROADLESS AREAS lie to either side of the Polaris-to-Wise River Road, offering excellent opportunities for hiking, skiing, wildlife watching, and off-highway vehicle use. Campgrounds and access trails throughout.

CHARCOAL KILNS located west of Interstate 15 at the Melrose interchange can be reached by Forest Road 187. The kilns were used from 1881 to 1900 to produce fuel for a copper smelter at Glendale.

WILDERNESS AREAS

LEE METCALF 108,000 acres on the Beaverhead include high alpine lakes, streams, and cirque basins. One unit of the wilderness is the rugged, highly glaciated Spanish Peaks Unit.

ANACONDA-PINTLER 72,537 acres located in the northwest corner of the forest. A beautiful mix of high peaks, glacial lakes, and open park lands, containing several species of trees.

RECREATIONAL OPPORTUNITIES

HIKING AND RIDING About half of the national forest's more than 1,600 miles of trails are well-marked and maintained. Fine day hiking and overnight opportunities in the East and West Pioneer mountains. Fine horseback riding opportunities in open, high country.

CAMPING Thirty campgrounds containing nearly 250 sites. Dispersed camping is allowed in much of the forest.

RECREATIONAL CABINS Twelve cabins available for rent during various times of the year. For more information, contact the Forest Supervisor's office.

SCENIC DRIVES The 60-mile Polaris-to-Wise River gravel loop road offers sweeping vistas of surrounding mountain ranges in Montana, Idaho, and Wyoming. Wonderful wildflower displays in mid-summer.

HUNTING Fine elk hunting, as well as mule deer, moose, pronghorn, black bear, and bighorn sheep.

FISHING More than one thousand miles of fishable streams and 150 high mountain lakes with fish.

ALPINE SKIING Maverick Mountain (one chair lift and one pony lift), located thirty-eight miles northwest of Dillon.

CROSS-COUNTRY SKIING Several marked trails throughout the forest, with particularly beautiful routes in the Pioneer Mountains.

SNOWMOBILING 168 miles of groomed snowmobile trails. Popular routes include the Virginia City-to-Clover Meadows trail in the Gravelly Range and the 35-mile trail from Polaris, in the Grasshopper Valley, to Wise River, in the Pioneer Mountains.

OFF-ROAD VEHICLES 824 miles of trail open to trail bikes. All trails outside of wilderness areas are open to mountain bikes. Several good routes for four-wheel-drive vehicles in the Tendoy Mountains and on the western edge of the Beaverhead along the Continental Divide near Frying Pan Creek.

ADMINISTRATIVE OFFICES

FOREST HEADQUARTERS 610 N. Montana St., Dillon, MT 59725 (406) 683-3900

MADISON RANGER DISTRICT 5 Forest Service Rd., Ennis, MT 59729 (406) 682-4253

WISDOM RANGER DISTRICT P.O. Box 236, Wisdom, MT 59761 (406) 689-3243

DILLON RANGER DISTRICT 610 N. Montana St., Dillon, MT 59725 (406) 683-3900

WISE RIVER RANGER DISTRICT P.O. Box 100, Wise River, MT 59762 (406) 832-3178

SHERIDAN RANGER DISTRICT P.O. Box 428, Sheridan, MT 59749 (406) 842-5432

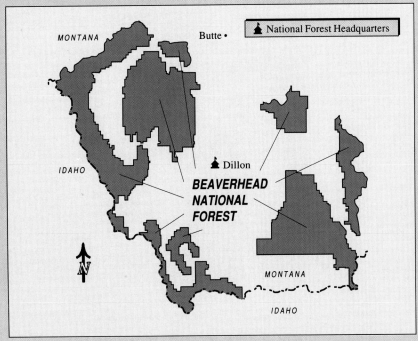

Autumn splashes the lower elevations of the Gallatin National Forest along Taylor Creek, a tributary of the Gallatin River. This season is an ideal time to drink in the abundant natural beauty of the Gallatin, though travelers in the backcountry must be prepared for early snows. ROB OUTLAW

Gallatin

The majesty of mountains

Of all the many natural splendors of the Gallatin National Forest — from its dancing rivers to its rich range of wildlife — its mountains may remain most firmly etched in the minds of those who visit. Whether they drink in the high country from the Gallatin's two thousand miles of trail or nearly one thousand miles of roadway, they will quickly realize why people have long waxed poetic about these highlands. "Traveled through some of the most beautiful mountain scenery of which it is possible for man to conceive," wrote W. E. Atchison, a gold seeker who in 1864 passed before the high, wild country lining the northern reaches of today's Gallatin National Forest. "It was beautiful rather than sublime, those mighty hills as they rise in gentle slopes away up toward the heavens covered with forests of pine and the verdure of summer."

The six mountain ranges that fill this southwest Montana national forest — the Bridger, Madison, Absaroka, Beartooth, Crazy, and Gallatin ranges — have shaped the lives of many who lived in or even passed through this region. For the Paleo-Indians who hunted game and gathered plants here ten thousand years ago, the scatter of high peaks was surely the source of profound mystery — the hiding place of summer thunder, the house of the winter winds. To a dogged bunch of nineteenth century gold miners like the poetic Mr. Atchison, the land held the promise of untold riches and high adventure. In the summer of 1877, a full decade after the wagon trains had stopped rolling along John Bozeman's trail to the Montana gold fields, the mountains along the southern edge of the Gallatin National Forest offered safe harbor for a band of Nez Perce Indians fleeing from the U.S. Cavalry. It was here, near present day Cooke City, that the great Chief Joseph deftly led seven hundred followers and two thousand horses on the last leg of what would turn into an epic — but futile — 1,700-mile run for the freedom of Canadian soil.

Horsemen move with the clouds across the rolling tundra of the Gallatin high country. Most of the national forest's trails are open to use by horses and other pack animals. DAVID TIPPETS

While today's visitor may not find quite the same level of human drama in the high country, the mountains of the Gallatin National Forest still have the ability to inspire and amaze. There is an unforgettable air of wildness here, where a rich mosaic of meadow lands is interspersed with stands of lodgepole and whitebark pine, Engelmann spruce, and subalpine fir. This mix is controlled in large measure by brief but brilliant summers and winters that lie cold and white over much of the higher landscape for eight months of the year. The sheer grandeur of this national forest, along with its close proximity to Yellowstone National Park, allows it to tally more than 2.2 million visitor days each year—more than any other national forest in Montana.

Recreational opportunities surround visitors to the Gallatin. The splendid folds of the Hyalite Peaks lie just a few miles south of the Gallatin's headquarters in Bozeman, for example. This area in the Gallatin Range takes its name from the mineral "hyalite," a colorless, often translucent opal that laces many of the high ridgelines here. Over countless centuries, ice, wind, and water have sliced the Hyalites into a dazzling array of stark hanging valleys and plunging waterfalls — an absolute paradise for every recreational taste. The Hyalites can provide anything from a gentle streamside walk to backpacking or mountain climbing trips of expedition proportions.

The Palisades Falls National Recreation Trail is one of seven such trails on the Gallatin National Forest.
MICHAEL S. SAMPLE

At the heart of this region lies Hyalite Reservoir, a two hundred-acre artificial lake capable of storing eight thousand acre-feet of water. The reservoir provides drinking water for the city of Bozeman, as well as irrigation water for much of the agricultural lands of the nearby Gallatin Valley. In summer, sailboarders waltz with the mountain winds that routinely pour across these waters, while fishermen ply the coves and bays, waiting for strikes of cutthroat trout and arctic grayling.

Through a cooperative effort with several community organizations in the region, the Hyalite drainage has become one of the most diverse and accessible national forest recreational centers in the state. It contains an excellent system of handicapped-accessible campgrounds, picnic grounds, and trails, including the beautiful West Shore and Langhor

The Bridger Mountains northeast of Bozeman are a striking collection of sedimentary buckles and limestone palisades, thought to be about 50 million years old. MICHAEL S. SAMPLE

THE NIGHT THE GALLATIN ROCKED

Most people tend to think of the great forces of nature that shaped the northern Rockies, such as the violent lava spews of the Yellowstone region and the slow, cold grind of glacial ice, as events anchored in some hazy, distant past. But on August 17, 1959, change came quickly and dramatically to a piece of the Gallatin National Forest. One minute there was only the stillness of a Montana summer night. The next, the earth was shaking and shuddering with a violence few people have ever seen. An enormous segment of Precambrian rock broke loose from its moorings on the south side of Madison Canyon and thundered across the valley with enough force to carry the leading edge more than 400 feet above the level of the Madison River. With the stream channel blocked, a lake began to form where none existed before. Large sections of roadway were buried under rubble or jolted completely off their beds. The north shore of Hebgen Reservoir sank, flooding cabins and sending a series of large standing waves crashing against the face of the dam. In less than a minute, 250 campers were trapped in the Madison River Canyon. Twenty-eight died there.

This earthquake along Red Canyon fault, measuring a staggering 7.1 on the Richter scale, was among the most significant ever felt in the Rocky Mountains. The initial shock, followed in subsequent weeks by smaller tremors, spread through eight western states and damaged buildings in every town within a one hundred-mile radius.

A massive slab of mountainside serves as mute testimony to the 1959 earthquake that rocked the Madison River Canyon, killing 28 people. Today, a 37,800-acre tract on the Gallatin National Forest has been set aside as a special study and interpretive area.
MICHAEL S. SAMPLE

One scientist compared the power of the quake to the explosion of 2,500 atomic bombs.

Today, the earthquake area can be visited by traveling along U.S. Highway 287 between Ennis and West Yellowstone, Montana. A Forest Service visitor center is located near the western edge of Quake Lake and contains a working seismograph, as well as dramatic photos of the earthquake aftermath. National forest camping is available in the immediate area at Beaver Creek and Cabin campgrounds, as well as on the south shore of Hebgen Lake.

It's easy to forget that the great mountain ranges of the Gallatin National Forest are dynamic, ever-changing places. Some of those changes flow gently across the land: fingers of water carving ever deeper through dark, tree-studded canyons, elk descending to winter range on the trailing edge of autumn. But sometimes, like on that August night in 1959, the changes rock the land. To witness such violent evolution can be terrifying. But this is, and likely always will be, the real legacy of the Rocky Mountains.

interpretive trails and a cool, easy pathway that leads to the feathery cascades of Grotto Falls. Two handicapped-accessible fishing sites are located along the northern reaches of Hyalite Canyon, while wheelchair-accessible fishing piers have been installed on the east shore of Hyalite Reservoir. Handicapped visitors also can rent Window Rock Cabin, a small field station built in the 1940s and now outfitted with a wheelchair ramp and special-access restroom facilities.

Mountain climbing is one of the most enticing experiences in the Hyalite area. Possible climbs range from relatively easy trail walks up Mount Blackmore, Big Chief Mountain, and Hyalite Peak to rugged scrambles up Chisholm Mountain and Boles Peak and rope-assisted ascents up the sheer bedrock slopes of Abbott and White mountains.

From atop any of these peaks soaring to heights of ten thousand feet, the land tumbles to the far horizons in a riot of mountainscapes. To the west lie the rugged crags of the Spanish Peaks. The sheer folds of these Precambrian rocks are dotted with dozens of glacial cirque lakes. When viewed from a high alpine perch, they shimmer in the sun like a handful of sapphires tossed down from the heavens. To the south and east from the Hyalites rise the high reaches of the Beartooths and the northern Absarokas, the latter providing the northern part of the area's grizzly range.

Rising to the northeast are the limestone ramparts of the Bridger Mountains, named for famed U.S. Army scout and frontiersman Jim Bridger, who punched a trail through this range to carry miners to the gold fields of Virginia City. And beyond the Bridgers, ripping out of a sea of grass thousands of feet into the blue Montana sky, are the fierce, isolated Crazy Mountains. High up in the Crazies, probably around 1858, a young Crow Indian named Plenty Coups cried and fasted for days to receive a vision. And a vision he got. In his dream, later interpreted by the tribal elder Yellow Bear, Plenty Coups was told that in his lifetime "the buffalo would go away forever and in their place on the plains will come the bulls and the calves of the white men."

Marsh marigolds bloom across wet meadows in the Absaroka-Beartooth Wilderness, on the Gallatin National Forest. Much of this stretch of wild lands borders Yellowstone National Park. DAN TYERS

Looking at this wild, unfettered country, it seems most appropriate that more than forty percent of the Gallatin's 1.7 million acres has been preserved in two congressionally designated wilderness areas. More than half of the Absaroka-Beartooth Wilderness is found on the Gallatin, while the remainder is split between Montana's Custer National Forest to the east and Wyoming's Shoshone National Forest to the south. The Absaroka-Beartooth is a dizzying mix of tundra and bold, stocky mountain peaks, many of which are rimmed by snow virtually every month of the year. The Gallatin also contains more than half of the 249,000-acre Lee Metcalf Wilderness, which it shares with the Beaverhead National Forest and the Bureau of Land Management. A large portion of the Lee Metcalf straddles the peaks of the Madison Range, a high huddle of 10,000-foot summits, most of which rise from exquisite braids of subalpine meadows. These mountains are comprised of igneous and metamorphic rocks dating back 2.7 billion years, covered by thick layers of sedimentary formations, the last of which were laid down by an inland sea a short time before the extinction of the dinosaurs. Even today, these mountains continue to heave toward the sky along active fault lines located at their southern and western edges — an excruciatingly slow and patient battle between the powers of uplift and the erosional forces of ice, wind, and water that would eventually level these peaks into a flat, featureless plain.

The large amount of wild land in the Gallatin, coupled with the adjacent 2.2 million acres of Yellowstone National Park, has made this national forest a haven for virtually every species of North American big game animal except the caribou. Bighorn sheep, grizzly bear, Rocky Mountain goat, moose, bison, black bear, mule deer, white-tailed deer, mountain lions, elk and, occasionally, pronghorn antelope all roam the region, along with a long list of birds, fish, and other smaller mammals — more than 325 species in all. The elk herds of the Gallatin are extremely impressive, providing some of the best hunting anywhere in the state.

Tufts of lupine and the bright gold of balsamroot flowers mean summer has arrived at Fox Creek Meadows in the Gallatin National Forest south of Bozeman. Indians throughout Montana ate the seeds, inner stems, and roots of the balsamroot. The lupine, while not edible, enriches mountain soils by taking in nitrogen from the air to manufacture food. ROB OUTLAW

Protecting these animals can, at times, seem like a complex game of chess. The needs of each species must be clearly understood, and then the resources must be managed in a way that allows for other uses of the national forest — from hiking and hunting to mining and the harvest of nearly 20 million board feet of timber each year.

More than half of the Gallatin's 1.7 million acres are located in the grizzly bear recovery zone — habitat considered crucial to the survival of this formidable creature. In recent years, the national forest has spent $50,000 to $75,000 a year just to manage the land for the benefit of this threatened species. Most of that money goes toward educating the public on ways to get along with the bear. At the start of a typical elk hunting season, for instance, Gallatin National Forest employees contact hundreds of hunting camps to advise hunters on the proper way to camp, hunt, clean, and pack out their kills without attracting a hungry grizzly.

Coyotes are just one of dozens of mammals living on Gallatin National Forest lands. While coyotes do occasionally feed on deer or even young cattle, far more often their diet consists of small rodents. W. PERRY CONWAY

Each year thousands of fishermen from around the country flock to the banks of the Gallatin River — one of three renowned fisheries on the Gallatin National Forest. DENVER A. BRYAN

The Gallatin National Forest also has worked with the Montana Department of Fish, Wildlife and Parks, the Rocky Mountain Elk Foundation, and the National Park Service to acquire more winter range habitat for the large number of elk that migrate north from Yellowstone National Park each winter. The need for more winter range has stemmed from the growth in the park's northern elk herd. The effort to acquire additional range has drawn the support of Congress and the public. Other cooperative efforts involving wildlife include the reintroduction of peregrine falcons, with the help of the Pergrine Fund, and a study of how moose are affected by fire, timber harvesting, elk populations, and fluctuations in food sources.

No discussion of the Gallatin's wildlife would be complete without mentioning the one resource that pulls more people to this forest from around the world than any other: its blue ribbon trout streams. The term "blue ribbon trout stream" is a nickname born in Montana thirty years ago, to identify segments of the state's waterways that were of "Class One" quality. Class One streams originally had to score high in four

areas: stream productivity, access, aesthetics, and fishing pressure. When the votes were in, portions of six Montana streams, totaling 452 miles, had made the grade. Fully half of those were in the Gallatin National Forest in the waters of the Madison, Gallatin, and Yellowstone rivers.

Twenty years later, the state Department of Fish, Wildlife and Parks re-evaluated Montana's rivers, based on a more sophisticated computerized inventory. Although this changed to a small degree the streams that qualified for Class One status, it did nothing to diminish the seal of approval earlier given to the Madison, Gallatin, and Yellowstone. These rivers have earned their status as world-class trout fisheries in large part because of their clean, cold waters, deep

---

A bull elk bugles the sun up on the Gallatin National Forest. Autumn bugling, which is really more a high-pitched whistling punctuated by a series of grunts, is a bull elk's way of announcing his territory. Often, such bugling will bring in other male challengers, which the bull may then have to stave off through a loud clash of antlers. GLENN VAN NIMWEGEN

pools, and gravel beds rich with insects. The Madison is known for its rainbow and brown trout populations, the Gallatin for rainbow trout, and the Yellowstone outside of the national park for cutthroats, browns, and rainbows.

Year after year and season after season, these rivers pour northward with all the wild magic of the Yellowstone country still in their waters. The Madison River alone, which carves a lovely northwestward course out of a land of dark, piney forests, holds two thousand to three thousand trout per mile in some places! Visitors who make their way into the mountains of the Gallatin also will find outstanding trout fishing in many of the high country lakes.

But a growing number of people look forward to the day when fall takes its last walk through the Gallatin, pulling the door shut on another year of fishing. These outdoor lovers have found that winter, with its brilliant skies and thick coverlets of snow, brings its own rich recreational rewards. Each year, thousands of downhill skiers head for the powder-laden slopes and chutes of Bridger Bowl, a resort operated on national forest lands under a special-use permit. Cross-country skiers flock to more than one hundred kilometers of ski trails, including the famed Rendezvous Ski Area near the town of West Yellowstone, where both the United States Ski Association and U.S. Biathlon Association train. Even more popular are snowmobiles. The Gallatin contains 426 miles of marked snowmobile trails, including the fabulous Big Sky Trail that runs from Bear Creek to Grayling Creek. A journey along the remote trail, while not to be taken lightly, each year gives thousands of snowmobilers an unforgettable glimpse into the rugged scenery and splendid wildlife of a northern Rocky Mountain winter. ■

Big Sky Resort, top right, while privately owned, is surrounded by Gallatin National Forest. Deep powder, short lift lines, and plenty of sunshine make both Big Sky and Bridger Bowl, northeast of Bozeman, exceptional ski resorts.
GARRY WUNDERWALD

The beautiful Bohemian waxwing, right, is a winter resident of the Gallatin National Forest. Waxwings get their name from the shiny red splotches that look like sealing wax on their secondary wing feathers. ALAN AND SANDY CAREY

GALLATIN
NATIONAL FOREST DIRECTORY

POINTS OF INTEREST

HYALITE PEAKS can be reached from Bozeman by Hyalite Canyon Road. Well-developed recreational facilities, including campgrounds, boat launching ramps, and a large network of trails leading through 155,000-acre Gallatin Range.

MADISON RIVER CANYON EARTHQUAKE AREA is located twelve miles northwest of West Yellowstone, Montana. Site of major earthquake in 1959. Visitor Center, twenty miles northwest of West Yellowstone, and self-guided auto tour.

GALLATIN PETRIFIED FOREST contains more than one hundred species of petrified trees distributed over forty square miles.

WILDERNESS AREAS

LEE METCALF 140,000 acres of the wilderness are on the Gallatin. Contains dense stands of spruce and Douglas-fir, as well as streams, waterfalls, high alpine peaks, and meadows.

ABSAROKA-BEARTOOTH 575,000 acres of the wilderness are on the Gallatin. High tundra dotted with hundreds of high alpine lakes.

RECREATIONAL ACTIVITIES

HIKING AND RIDING Two thousand miles of riding and hiking trails located throughout the forest, with more than eight hundred miles in the Lee Metcalf and Absaroka-Beartooth wilderness areas. Seven National Recreation Trails.

CAMPING Thirty-seven developed campgrounds, most open until the middle of September. No tent camping near West Yellowstone due to grizzlies. Dispersed camping allowed in much of the forest.

RECREATIONAL CABINS Available for rent during various times of the year. For more information, contact the Ranger District offices.

SCENIC DRIVES U.S Highway 191 south from Bozeman toward West Yellowstone passes through a striking canyon of Precambrian basement rock spattered with quartz, feldspar, hornblende, and mica. U.S. Highway 89 south of Livingston to Gardiner and Yellowstone National Park passes through Paradise Valley, a wide forest floor bounded on one side by the Absaroka Mountains and on the other by the Gallatin Mountains.

KAYAKING AND RAFTING Whitewater kayaking and rafting on the Yellowstone River north of Gardiner, and kayaking on the Gallatin River south of Bozeman.

HUNTING Elk, deer, bighorn sheep, mountain goat, moose, and black bear.

FISHING One thousand miles of streams, as well as reservoirs and hundreds of high country lakes. Renowned fisheries on the Gallatin, Madison, and Yellowstone rivers.

ALPINE SKIING Bridger Bowl, sixteen miles northeast of Bozeman (five chair lifts and one rope tow) and Big Sky Resort, on private lands along U.S. Highway 191 south of Bozeman (two gondolas, five chair lifts, and one rope tow).

CROSS-COUNTRY SKIING One hundred kilometers of trails throughout the forest, with excellent opportunities in the West Yellowstone and Cooke City areas. Marked trails adjacent to the Big Sky Resort. Thirty-one kilometers of groomed trails and fifteen kilometers of non-groomed trails in the Rendezvous Winter Sports Area, just south of West Yellowstone, the training center for U.S. and many international ski teams.

SNOWMOBILING Ten individual public snowmobiling areas on the forest, with 426 miles of marked trails. Two hundred miles of groomed trials tie into trails going into Yellowstone National Park and Idaho, including the Two Top National Recreation Trail leading to Two Top Mountain.

OFF-ROAD VEHICLES Four-wheeled vehicle opportunities available, largely on primitive roads. Consult the travel map or local Ranger District office.

ADMINISTRATIVE OFFICES

FOREST HEADQUARTERS Box 130, Federal Building, Bozeman, MT 59771 (406) 587-6701

BOZEMAN RANGER DISTRICT 601 Nikles, Bozeman, MT 59715 (406) 587-6920

BIG TIMBER RANGER DISTRICT P.O. Box A, Big Timber, MT 59011 (406) 932-5155

LIVINGSTON RANGER DISTRICT Route 62, Box 3197, Livingston, MT 59047 (406) 222-1892

HEBGEN RANGER DISTRICT P.O. Box 520, West Yellowstone, MT 59758 (406) 646-7369

GARDINER RANGER DISTRICT P.O. Box 5, Gardiner, MT 59030 (406) 848-7375

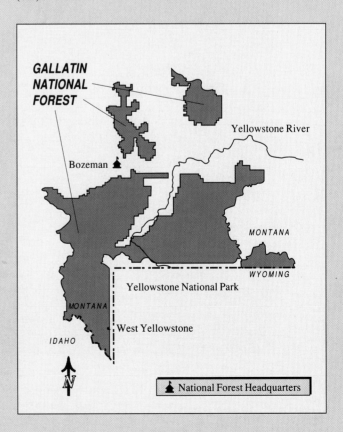

First light comes to the top of Montana, in the magnificent Beartooth Mountains. In the upper left is 12,799-foot Granite Peak — the highest mountain in the state. Twenty-seven other peaks in the Beartooth Mountains scrape the sky at over twelve thousand feet. MICHAEL S. SAMPLE

Custer

Wide
reaches
of grandeur

Perhaps none of the wild, yawning reaches of national forest in Montana contains more surprises than the one that takes its name from George Armstrong Custer — the brazen, blond-haired general who met his maker in 1876 on a grassy hillside above the Little Bighorn River. The 1.2 million-acre Custer National Forest is comprised not of one giant tract of land, but of widely scattered pockets of both mountain and plain. Together these lands stretch for more than 650 miles, from the bright alpine slopes of the Rockies to the dark folds of the Black Hills, from the icy cap of Granite Peak (Montana's highest mountain, at 12,799 feet) to a flat, lazy braid of grass and hardwoods along the Sheyenne River in eastern North Dakota.

These parcels of Custer National Forest make a fine journey for visitors to southcentral and southeast Montana, who can wander slowly and deliberately through each region. Their trip might begin south of Red Lodge, on the extreme western fringes of the forest. Here one finds portions of the magnificent Beartooth Plateau — roughly eighty thousand acres of rolling alpine tundra and sparkling lakes, much of it hovering more than six thousand feet above the plains below.

Few people who cross this vast stretch of unbroken high country ever forget it, whether they travel by foot along one of several national forest trails or by car along the Beartooth Highway (U.S. Highway 212).

This soaring, breath-taking road connects Red Lodge with Cooke City and Silver Gate, two small communities at the northeast entrance to Yellowstone National Park. Travelers on this route, which was recently designated a National Forest Scenic Byway, literally roll across the top of the world. After climbing sharply out of Rock Creek Canyon, the highway continues south, leaving the Custer National Forest for the state of Wyoming at an elevation of 10,350 feet. By contrast, the much-celebrated Going-to-the-Sun Highway in Glacier National Park reaches its greatest height crossing Logan Pass, at just 6,664 feet. After driving the Beartooth Highway in the 1970s, well-seasoned CBS travel reporter Charles Kuralt pronounced it "the most beautiful highway in America."

The geological story behind the formation of the Beartooth Plateau is one of staggering force and proportion. The rock underlying most of this high sweep of tundra — much of it streaky, coarse-grained slabs of metamorphic rock known as gneiss — is thought to have been brewed deep within the earth more than 3 billion years ago, making it among the oldest rock in the American West. Long after these rocks were formed, a great collision occurred along several fault lines, or cracks in the earth's crust. As the land masses collided, the Beartooth Plateau was squeezed slowly upward. Inch by inch it climbed, ripping through layers of much younger, softer sedimentary rock and finally coming to rest perhaps as much as twenty thousand feet above where it once lay.

No sooner had the land begun to rise than erosional forces began to tear it away, piece by tiny piece. In fact, glaciers sculpted much of this landscape long after the main uplift of the Beartooths had ground to a halt. With a layer of rock debris clutched tightly in their cold

A blanket of green covers the foot of the North Face of the Beartooth Mountains. Once the province of fur trappers and explorers, the Beartooths still hold plenty of adventure for climbers, backpackers, hunters, and fishermen. MICHAEL S. SAMPLE

bellies, these mammoth sheets of ice ground across mountain peaks and down stream valleys, carving a magnificent tapestry of hanging valleys and U-shaped canyons in the process. Hikers in Custer's Beartooth-Absaroka Wilderness can thank these great tongues of ice for the stunning vistas that await them from the crest of Sundance Pass, from Silver Run and Sylvan peaks, and from the cold blue waters of the Snow Lakes. Though glaciation is a slow phenomenon, with the ice often advancing only inches per day, the sculpting effect in the Beartooths is as dramatic as if the mountains had been no more than mounds of ice cream, cut by the sweep of a hot metal scoop.

Today, with the bulk of glacial ice melted away and the ten high plateaus of the region carpeted with alpine clover, phlox, Ross'geum, and forget-me-nots, the western edge of the Custer National Forest is revered by outdoor recreationists around the world. More than two dozen trailheads provide access to these mountains, offering the visitor opportunities ranging from a warm spring stroll through arid

Visitors to the Beartooth District of the Custer National Forest will see a multitude of wildflowers, including the beautiful white phlox. Cultivated versions of this flower adorn gardens throughout America. The wild variety blooms along the Beartooth trails in June and July.
ROB OUTLAW

The Beartooth and Absaroka mountains, top, contain hundreds of lakes to enjoy and explore. Many also contain good populations of golden, cutthroat, rainbow, brook, and brown trout. ERWIN AND PEGGY BAUER

Clark's Fork Canyon to a Fourth of July ski trip along the upper reaches of the Beartooth Plateau, from big game hunting of bighorn sheep and Rocky Mountain goat to morning photo forays along the steely waters of Glacier, Moon, and Sliderock lakes.

Thousands of people come to the Beartooths with fishing rods, searching for cutthroat, golden brook, rainbow, brown, and lake trout, as well as arctic grayling, in the hundreds of lakes here. Others come to climb mountains, embarking across tundra trails to the slopes of Mount Rearguard and Thunder Mountain, as well any of two dozen other peaks in the Beartooths that lie above twelve thousand feet. Rock climbers head for the sheer slopes cradling the West Rosebud and East Rosebud rivers, while the slow winter flow of water down beautiful Silver Falls, along the Lake Fork of Rock Creek, makes it a perfect destination for ice climbers.

The thick cloak of solitude that wraps so many of the trails and streamsides here belies the extreme popularity of the region. The 944,060-acre Absaroka-Beartooth Wilderness is the third most visited wilderness area in the United States. That popularity can be explained by a single visit to the edge of one of its dazzling, dizzying vistas or just one close brush with the bighorn sheep or Rocky Mountain goats that routinely amble past these high, bony fingers of rock.

Most people come to admire the Beartooths for their sheer, unbridled beauty, but many geologists marvel at this range for a different reason. A band of igneous

A grand swell of alpine tundra caps the 10,000-foot Hellroaring Plateau, southwest of Red Lodge. Like most of the plateaus in the Beartooths, Hellroaring is dotted with beautiful alpine lakes, many of which hold fine populations of golden, brook, and cutthroat trout. DAVID MUENCH

SAVING THE WILDERNESS

Just a decade ago, the hundreds of thousands of people who visited the Absaroka-Beartooth Wilderness each year were literally loving the place to death. Soapsuds polluted streams and lakes. Dozens of lake shores and stream corridors were trampled, resulting in the death of large numbers of trees. Garbage littered the trails. Hikers cut extra pathways into hillsides and across meadows, causing erosion that would take decades to heal. Although these problems stemmed more from ignorance than maliciousness, they were nonetheless changing the face of the backcountry at a frightening pace. With use on the Absaroka-Beartooth expected to increase significantly, Custer National Forest personnel wondered how the human impacts could be lessened in the years ahead.

Some believed limiting the number of visitors was the only solution. But wilderness managers on the Beartooth Ranger District of the Custer National Forest decided to tackle the project from another direction—education. Beginning in 1979, forestry technicians began teaching a "no-trace" class to, among others, sixth-grade students in schools throughout the area. The course was carefully designed to teach kids how to make their way through the wilderness without a trace, much as Indians and mountain men did 150 years ago.

The no-trace message has been delivered to more than sixteen thousand students now. In recent years, the program has reached eighteen to twenty percent of the total sixth-grade population in Montana.

Has all this hard work paid off? Without question, say instructors Blase Dilulo and Tom Alt. "There was a time when I felt more like a garbage collector than a wilderness ranger," says Dilulo. "A good backpack wouldn't last me more than two years, simply because it was always so crammed full of trash. Today I can walk thirty miles of wilderness trail and only pick up a handful of litter. And no longer do you see fire rings all over the place, or find fish entrails lying along the shores of our lakes."

Some of this program's success can be tied to the fact that residents from the three counties surrounding the Absaroka-Beartooth Wilderness —including the greater Billings area—make up a significant portion of its users. A young person hiking one of these trails today could well be a former student of a Custer National Forest no-trace class.

The success of the Custer no-trace program is making resource managers take a second look at the idea of using education to solve land-use problems.

Trout are plentiful in the lakes and streams of the high alpine plateaus in the Beartooths. Because weather in this country can turn nasty virtually any month of the year, backcountry anglers should be certain to have adequate clothing. ROB OUTLAW

rocks known as the Stillwater Complex lies along the northern edge of these mountains. Stacked like thin layers of cake, these rocks are extremely rich in minerals, including nickel, iron, copper, palladium, and platinum, as well as eighty percent of America's known reserves of chrome. In fact, only two other such mineral complexes exist in the entire world — in Russia and South Africa. Mining of the Stillwater Complex for copper goes back to the latter part of the nineteenth century. But mining there began in earnest during World War II, when German U-boats began gaining control of the shipping lanes and threatened America's sources of various strategic metals.

Today the eastern edge of the Stillwater Complex, near the town of Nye, is mined for platinum and palladium — rare metals used in everything from electronics to the manufacture of catalytic converters. In addition, technology has advanced enough in recent years to make the extraction and processing of the abundant low-grade chromium deposits here profitable. It's likely only a matter of time before companies throughout North America submit proposals for the mining of this chromium.

Leaving the Beartooth Plateau by driving north along the Beartooth Highway, travelers can see a long, gentle range of mountains off to the east, just before the road begins its headlong tumble into the ice-scoured throat of Rock Creek Canyon. The range

climbs easily out of a high plain cloaked in ragged tufts of sage. These are the Pryor Mountains, which — like the nearby river and town — took their name from Sergeant Nathaniel Pryor of the Lewis and Clark expedition. However, another member of that famed group of intrepid explorers — John Colter — actually became the first to a traverse the foothills of the Pryors. On a fantastic 500-mile trek in the dead of winter, Colter made his way through the Pryor River country into the Bighorns, southwest to the pinnacles of the Tetons, and then back north past the hot pots of Yellowstone National Park — the first white man to ever set eyes on much of what is now considered the finest of the western wonderlands.

The tracks of John Colter's snowshoes have long since faded from the Pryor Mountain country. But signs left by people who lived in this remote stretch of the Custer National Forest long before the arrival of European explorers are still intact, hidden in the twisted maze of limestone canyons and caves that dot these solitary, hauntingly beautiful highlands.

Custer National Forest's Pryor Mountains and the adjacent Bureau of Land Management areas hold a diverse archaeological record. Researchers estimate the area contains well over one thousand cultural sites. Three times that number may exist on the entire national forest. Indeed, the chance of rounding a bend of trail in the Pryors and coming face to face with a

The elusive mountain lion, top, is one of the Custer National Forest's more magnificent residents. The animal was once hunted as a pest, but today is considered a valuable part of the wild fabric of the American West. JEFF FOOTT

In winter, the Beartooth Mountains, left, become a dazzling wonderland, with superb opportunities for cross-country skiing. MICHAEL S. SAMPLE

piece of prehistory thousands of years old gives this portion of the Custer an enduring appeal. Striking pictographs, many telling ancient tales of hunts for sheep and bison, decorate the walls of limestone caves. Crumbling remains of wooden structures built in the middle of the seventeeth century, whose uses are still unknown, are found along the high limestone ridges. Rings of stones used by Crow Indians and others to anchor the skirts of their tipis remain in place. Hikers along Bad Pass Trail will find old rock cairns, some of which served as pathway markers for nearly two thousand years, guiding the feet of countless Indians back and forth from the Yellowstone River Valley to the Bighorn Basin.

Today's traveler must plan a trip to the Pryor Mountains. These are remote, quiet mountains, with

Prairie falcons nest in the pine hills of the Custer National Forest near Ashland, left. Able to fly at speeds in excess of 150 miles per hour, these falcons will occasionally take another bird in flight, although most of their meals consist of ground squirrels and other small rodents. KRISTI DUBOIS

A lonesome lookout, below, rises above the timber on Yager Butte, southeast of Ashland. A Montana forest ranger developed a platform lookout in 1929 that could be built for one-third to one-fifth the cost of other structures in use at the time. Many of these are still standing, and a few are still used for fire suppression efforts. LARRY MAYER

most of the range cut only by a handful of rugged gravel roads. Those who do brave the dust and ruts to come here will find a variety of habitats, from dusky blankets of black sage along the lower edges of the national forest to 8,000-foot meadows bedecked with wildflowers. Visitors see few other people as they trek across these high shoulders and twisted, fossil-laden canyons, but they do stand a good chance of spotting mule deer, blue grouse, black bear, mountain lion, or, in the eastern Pryors, an occasional herd of wild horses. Many of the remote jeep roads along the eastern and southern fringe of the Pryors, incidentally, are perfect places for the adventurous mountain biker.

Continuing eastward, travelers drift across gently rolling country, endless acres of grass shimmering under a big blue splash of Montana sky. By the time they hit the next section of Custer National Forest near Ashland, the land has puckered into a collage of twisted ravines and rounded hummocks draped in ponderosa pine. This is cattle country, and has been for well over one hundred years. In fact, the blend of climate and soils provides an almost ideal setting for growing grass — a fact that has turned the Custer National Forest into the largest forage producer of any national forest in the United States.

The Ashland district is also well-known for wild animals found in its reaches. Each year, thousands of hunters make pilgrimages to this part of the national forest, beckoned by some of largest, most robust white-tailed deer, mule deer, and wild turkey populations in the northern Rockies.

Photographers, horseback riders, and wildlife watchers will find especially good outings in the Cook Mountain, King Mountain, and Tongue River Breaks Riding and Hiking areas. These three areas contain forty thousand acres of remote, untrammeled beauty, visited by few people and crossed by few developed trails. With only a handful of steps — perhaps up Hole in the Wall Creek or Gooseberry Draw — visitors can be wrapped in the kind of sweet, hushed world that makes the western national forests such places of solitude and recreation. A remarkable amount of the

The gentle green swells of the Long Pines in spring are rich in wildlife. Several roads traverse this lovely region near the Montana-North Dakota border. KRISTI DUBOIS

Ashland district forest has that kind of easy warmth about it — from the long, lazy vistas of Poker Jim Lookout to the rippling seas of grass that pour across the plains from the feet of Diamond Butte.

The Sioux Ranger District is the final stop on the Montana portion of the Custer National Forest. Here, eight tracts of land spill across southeast Montana and into northwest South Dakota. Sandwiched between the flows of the Little Missouri River and Box Elder Creek, this district is a loose weave of grassy hills and massive limestone towers, cushioned here and there by long, mellow ridgelines and ravines filled with squawbush, horsemint, and wild rose. Meadowlarks and loggerhead shrikes ride on the prairie winds, along with a host of raptors that can take the most experienced bird watchers by surprise. The Sioux Ranger District, in fact, contains the second-highest density of raptors in the United States, behind Idaho's Birds of Prey Refuge. This is a particularly good place to see merlins, turkey vultures, and golden eagles, as well as rough-legged and red-tailed hawks.

There is actually much more to the Custer National Forest. It continues to hopscotch across the plains to the east and southeast of the Montana state line, framing the badlands of Theodore Roosevelt National Park, running across the long reach of North Dakota almost to the Minnesota border. Long before most visitors leave the Montana units of the Custer, however, they understand well why writer John Steinbeck became so sentimental when he made a similar trip through the southeast and southcentral part of the state more than three decades ago. "It seems to me," he wrote in *Travels With Charley*, "that Montana is a great splash of grandeur. The land is rich with color, and the mountains are the kind I would create if mountains were ever put on my agenda." Steinbeck's words would have held true had he never set foot outside of the Custer National Forest. ■

The summit of Sundance Mountain in the Custer National Forest soars to an elevation of 12,272 feet. Sundance rises above the West Fork of Rock Creek.   MICHAEL S. SAMPLE

CUSTER
NATIONAL FOREST DIRECTORY

POINTS OF INTEREST

BEARTOOTH PLATEAU is a spectacular, alpine tundra environment northeast of Yellowstone National Park that can be entered by several wilderness trails along the Beartooth Face, northwest and southwest of Red Lodge. Location of Grasshopper Glacier, where millions of a now-extinct species of grasshopper are frozen in glacial ice.

PRYOR MOUNTAINS are a remote collection of limestone mountains ranging in height from about three thousand feet to more than eight thousand feet. Extremely rich in archaeological sites.

WILDERNESS AREAS

ABSAROKA-BEARTOOTH 345,694 acres of the wilderness are on the Custer. Rugged mountains, alpine tundra, lakes, streams, and steep canyons.

RECREATIONAL ACTIVITIES

HIKING AND RIDING Most trails located on the Beartooth Ranger District. A small number of quiet, remote paths can be found on the Pryor Mountain District and on the Ashland District, in the King Mountain, Cook Mountain, and Tongue River Breaks Hiking and Riding areas.

CAMPING Twenty-six developed campgrounds. Dispersed camping allowed on most of the forest.

RECREATIONAL CABINS Whitetail Cabin, eighteen miles east of Ashland, is available year-round. For more information, contact the Ashland Ranger District office.

SCENIC DRIVES U.S. Highway 212 (the Beartooth Highway) from Red Lodge to Cooke City across the Beartooth Plateau is a National Forest Scenic Byway.

KAYAKING Limited access on the Stillwater River from Woodbine Campground, an area recommended for experts only.

HUNTING A variety of big game, with deer and upland birds found on all forest districts. Bighorn sheep, elk, and Rocky Mountain goat are common on the Beartooth Ranger District, while the Ashland Ranger District has an excellent spring turkey season and white-tailed and mule deer hunting in the fall.

FISHING Hundreds of lakes and streams, primarily on the Beartooth Ranger District, provide habitat for cutthroat, golden, rainbow, brook, and lake trout.

ALPINE SKIING Red Lodge Mountain (five chair lifts, one rope tow, and one mitey-mite), west of Red Lodge.

CROSS-COUNTRY SKIING Lake Fork and Silver Run trails on the Beartooth Ranger District. Camps Pass on the Ashland Ranger District, east of Ashland.

SNOWMOBILING U.S. Highway 212 (Beartooth Highway), south of Red Lodge to Cooke City, is recommended for experts only.

OFF-ROAD VEHICLES Limited access in the Pryor Mountains, on existing roads only.

MOUNTAIN BIKES Pryor Mountains on existing roads, as well as roads and trails on the Beartooth Ranger District outside of the wilderness, with the exception of West Rosebud and Glacier Lake trails.

ADMINISTRATIVE OFFICES

FOREST HEADQUARTERS 2602 First Ave. N., P.O. Box 2556, Billings, MT 59103 (406) 657-6361

SIOUX RANGER DISTRICT Box 37, Camp Crook, SD 57724 (605) 797-4432

ASHLAND RANGER DISTRICT P.O. Box 168, Ashland, MT 59003 (406) 784-2344

BEARTOOTH RANGER DISTRICT Route 2, Box 3420, Red Lodge, MT 59068 (406) 446-2103

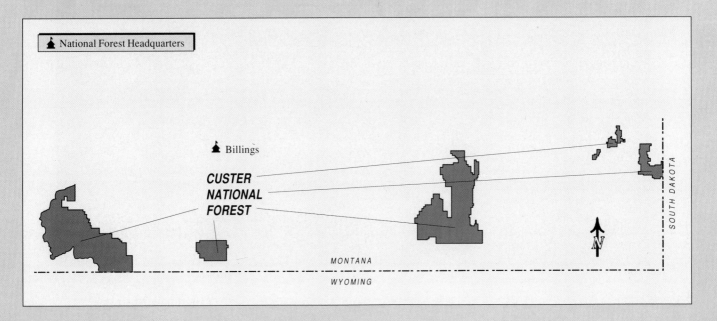

The morning sun clears the high peaks of the Swan Range in the Flathead National Forest. The view is from the Mission Mountains Wilderness, one of the most popular wilderness areas in Montana's national forests. MICHAEL S. SAMPLE

Conclusion

Hard choices ahead

Montana's national forests have long undergone natural processes that bring about change — fire, insects, disease, and even earthquakes. But new kinds of changes, wrought by humans, may in the long run be far more consequential.

For instance, thousands of out-of-state hunters are discovering the unsurpassed quality of Montana's big game herds. As a result, private landowners adjacent to the national forests have found they can make lucrative lease arrangements with hunting guides for the exclusive use of their lands during hunting season. In a typical case, a rancher may charge $3,000 to $3,500 for each elk taken from his property. Half of that amount goes to the outfitter, the other half to the landowner. That kind of money can easily make all the difference between being able to run a cattle ranch in the black or continuing to run it on the ragged edge of red. But these leases often cut off all access to the national forest lands that lie beyond the private property. The arrangements have resulted in such access problems on the Gallatin National Forest that officials there spend hundreds of hours each month trying to work out land trades, purchases, or other alternatives to restore public thoroughfares.

The increasing demand for recreation on Montana's national forests poses another problem. Most recreationists — whether backpackers or motorcyclists — simply don't want their playgrounds lined with clearcuts, mine tailings, or oil drilling pads. A growing segment of the public feels the Forest Service should do more to accommodate recreation and wildlife and less for extractive industries, such as timber companies. At the same time, strong pressure is coming from Washington to increase the number of trees cut on the region. Occasionally, such differences can be worked out among opposing factions, as was demonstrated recently in the historic set of meetings on the Deerlodge National Forest. But such compromise is still much more the exception than the rule. For the foreseeable future, the courts often will continue to decide what paths the national forests will take.

Thankfully, not all the changes occurring on Montana's national forests are so complicated or potentially explosive. One of the most positive new trends of the past few years has been the proliferation of cost-share programs, in which the Forest Service is able to complete important projects on national forest lands with money and labor contributed by private organizations. Thousands of acres of wildlife habitat have been improved with the financial support of the Rocky Mountain Elk Foundation. Much-needed handicapped-accessible recreational facilities have been built with the help of area Lion's Clubs, Boy Scout troops, and other civic organizations. Major contributions from Ducks Unlimited have improved crucial riparian habitats. Local snowmobile clubs have helped restore old backcountry field stations, which the Forest Service rents to the public for a nominal fee.

Montana's national forests represent what is arguably the greatest assemblage of scenery, solitude, and wildlife remaining anywhere in the American West. Even so, it's clear that these lands will undergo trying times in the years ahead — times that may challenge the very foundation of Gifford Pinchot's dream of multiple use. No easy solutions exist. The future will be a time for careful choices, for coming to grips with the real significance of these last, vast quilts of nature. ∎

A lodgepole pine seedling springs from charred ground after a forest fire, far left. Fires play an important role in lodgepole reproduction. The heat from a fire triggers the pine cones to open, releasing seeds.
STEVE WIRT

Blue grouse find a home in all of Montana's ten national forests. Males, such as the one at left, perform a colorful courtship display each spring that includes strutting and a series of low, muffled, booming or hooting notes.
GLENN VAN NIMWEGEN

HELPING YOUR FAVORITE NATIONAL FOREST

National forests educate as well as entertain. With books, brochures, maps, signs, exhibits, and self-guided trails, each national forest teaches visitors about its natural and cultural history and its resource management activities. What many visitors don't know is that much of this interpretive material comes from private organizations, not the Forest Service.

Interpretive associations are non-profit groups that work closely with the national forests to provide many interpretive services. Some associations fund interpretive specialists in national forests. Some

set up exhibits and interpretive trail signs. Some sell books, maps, and T-shirts and use profits to pay for different interpretive projects.

Faced with budget constraints and limited personnel, the Forest Service might have to skip some of these projects without the help of the interpretive associations. If you would like to find out more about these groups — or volunteer to help your favorite national forest — contact the following organizations:

Glacier Natural History Association
(Flathead National Forest)

West Glacier, MT 59936
Phone: (406) 888-5441

Pacific Northwest National Parks and Forests Association
(Beaverhead, Bitterroot, Deerlodge, Helena, Kootenai, Lewis and Clark, and Lolo national forests)
83 South King Street, Suite 212
Seattle, WA 98104
Phone: (206) 442-7958

Yellowstone Association for Natural Science, History, and Education
(Custer and Gallatin national forests)
Yellowstone National Park, WY 82190
Phone: (307) 344-7381

Spectacular scenery attracts visitors to Montana's national forests in all seasons. A cross-country skier, left, travels deep into the backcountry of the Gallatin National Forest during a mid-winter expedition. In the summer, the same route will be taken by hikers and horseback riders. Numerous scenic roads offer motorized access to all national forest visitors. GEORGE WUERTHNER

Perfect Companions to Montana National Forests

NEW! *The Montana Wildlife Viewing Guide*

by Carol and Hank Fischer

Where has all the wildlife gone? Nowhere.
It's all around us—you just need the *Montana Wildlife Viewing Guide* to show you where to look. This new book describes 113 wildlife viewing sites all across Montana, including Glacier and Yellowstone national parks. See eagles, bear, bison, and more—all from your car!

- 104 pages
- 40 full-color photos
- locator maps
- driving directions

- species found at each site
- fascinating wildlife facts
- outdoor recreation
- and much, much more!

6 x 9'', $5.95 softcover

Ask about our other Wildlife Viewing Guides on Idaho, Oregon, Utah, and Alberta.

The Hiker's Guide to Montana

by Bill Schneider   REVISED! Third Edition

For the hiker, Montana probably has more to offer than any other state. There are famous hiking areas such as Glacier National Park, the Beartooth Plateau, and the Mission Mountains. But even more significant are the dozens of hidden, almost unknown mountain ranges with outstanding scenery, fishing, climbing, and other rewards—places where you can hike all day without seeing another hiker.

The Hiker's Guide to Montana covers both the well-known and the uncelebrated mountain ranges—100 hikes in all!

Detailed topographic maps and photos complement the trail descriptions and complete the book.

Whether you're an experienced hiker or a rookie, *The Hiker's Guide to Montana* is loaded with new adventures for you.

6 x 9'', $9.95 softcover

More books about America's National Forests

The National Forests of America Series

Each book in this series focuses on the national forests of one state or region, and features informative text, more than 100 outstanding color photos, helpful maps, and a directory to each national forest's recreational opportunities. Don't miss *California National Forests, Greater Yellowstone National Forests*, and *Washington National Forests*, and be sure to watch for others in this series.

128 pages, 8½ x 11'', $14.95 softcover

The National Forests Calendar

This is the first calendar devoted exclusively to America's national forests. This unique wall calendar features 15 striking color photos from national forests all across the country. Informative captions highlight the tremendous diversity of landscapes, wildlife, and outdoor recreation in the national forests.

24 pages, 12 x 9'', $7.95

To order these books and calendars, call toll free, 1-800-582-BOOK (have your VISA, MC handy), or send a check or money order along with $1.75 postage and handling for each book to Falcon Press, P.O. Box 1718, Helena, MT 59624.

Ask for our free catalog which includes a choice selection of recreational guidebooks, beautiful geographic books in full color, gorgeous wildlife and scenic calendars, and a lot more!